The Dark Night of Resistance

DANIEL BERRIGAN

The
Dark Night of
Resistance

WIPF & STOCK · Eugene, Oregon

To Bill and Tony
for I was homeless
and you gave me shelter

Wipf and Stock Publishers
199 W 8th Ave, Suite 3
Eugene, OR 97401

The Dark Night of Resistance
By Berrigan, Daniel
Copyright©1971 by Berrigan, Daniel
ISBN 13: 978-1-55635-469-4
ISBN 10: 1-55635-469-X
Publication date 5/7/2007
Previously published by Doubleday, 1971

SERIES FOREWORD

Daniel Berrigan is one of the most influential American Catholics of the twentieth century. A Jesuit priest, poet, and peacemaker, he has inspired countless people of faith and conscience to pursue the gospel vision of a world without war or nuclear weapons. Born in 1921, he entered the Society of Jesus in 1939, was ordained in 1952, and in 1957 published his first book of poetry, *Time Without Number*, which won the prestigious Lamont Poetry Award.

Since then Daniel Berrigan, my friend and Jesuit brother, has published over fifty books, including the award-winning play, *The Trial of the Catonsville Nine* (1970); an autobiography, *To Dwell in Peace* (1987); and many journals, essays, poetry collections, and scripture commentaries. Dan maintained close friend friendships with Thomas Merton and Dorothy Day. He also co-founded the Catholic Peace Fellowship and Clergy and Laity Concerned about Vietnam. But because of his early peace work, church authorities banished him to Latin America in 1966 and 1967. In early 1968, he traveled to Hanoi with Howard Zinn to experience firsthand the horrors of U.S. war-making and to rescue three U.S. soldiers who had been captured.

On May 19, 1968, with his brother Philip and other friends, he burned military draft files using homemade napalm in Catonsville, Maryland—an action which galvanized millions against the Vietnam war. For this creative nonviolence, Dan was tried, convicted, and sentenced to years in prison. In April of 1970, however, he went underground, eluding the FBI, and continued to draw widespread attention to his antiwar message. He was finally arrested in August, and imprisoned in Danbury, Connecticut until February 1972.

He continued to write and speak against war and nuclear weapons throughout the 70s. On September 9, 1980, both he and Philip participated in the first Plowshares Action, a protest at the General Electric Plant at King of Prussia, Pennsylvania. He faced ten years in prison, but was eventually sentenced to time served.

Since the early 1970s, Dan has lived in New York City with his Jesuit community. He continues to give lectures, conduct retreats, publish books of poetry and scripture study—and get arrested for his protests against war, injustice, and nuclear weapons. He remains a clear voice of resistance to war, gospel nonviolence, and peace for humanity.

Throughout his faithful, peacemaking life, Daniel Berrigan has consistently said no to every war, injustice, and weapon of violence. And with every no he accepts the cost. And he does not give up. Nominated many times for the Nobel Peace Prize, Dan often finds himself with friends before some judge and sitting on ice in some dismal holding cell. Such is the mark of a prophet, the sign of an apostle of peace.

"We have assumed the name of peacemakers," Dan writes in *No Bars to Manhood*,

> but we have been, by and large, unwilling to pay any significant price. And because we want the peace with half a heart and half a life and will, the war, of course, continues, because the waging of war, by its nature, is total—but the waging of peace, by our own cowardice, is partial. There is no peace because there are no peacemakers. There are no makers of peace because the making of peace is at least as costly as the making of war, at least as exigent, at least as disruptive, at least as liable to bring disgrace and prison and death in its wake.

"The only message I have to the world is: we are not allowed to kill innocent people," he told the court during his Plowshares Eight trial.

> We are not allowed to be complicit in murder. We are not allowed to be silent while preparations for mass murder proceed in our name, with our money, secretly. . . . It's terrible for me to live in a time where I have nothing to say to human beings except, 'Stop killing.' There are other beautiful things that I would love to be saying to people. There are other projects I could be very helpful at. And I can't do them. I cannot. Because everything is endangered. Everything is up for grabs. Ours is a kind of primitive situation, even though we would call ourselves sophisticated. Our plight is very primitive from a Christian point of view. We are back where we started. 'Thou shalt not kill'; we are not allowed to kill. Everything today comes down to that—everything.

I am very grateful to Wipf and Stock Publishers for republishing some of Dan's classic works in a series, books which influenced millions of people when they first appeared. I hope these books will be studied, passed around to friends and neighbors, and promoted far and wide. They still offer great hope, wisdom, and encouragement.

In the life and words of Daniel Berrigan we discover new faith in the God of peace and courage to pursue God's reign of peace. We see signs and guideposts for the path ahead, toward a new future of peace. And we find strength to take our own stand for justice and disarmament, to take another step forward on the road to peace and nonviolence. May these books inspire us to become, like Daniel Berrigan, peacemakers in a world of war.

—John Dear
Cerrillos, New Mexico
August 2007

Contents

The Dark Night of Resistance

April 1970

I start these notes quite literally on the run. In town, the spring is breaking out in a cataclysm—unexpected! as though in midwinter, dark and pandemic, a healing had been found. I walk down streets like a shadow or cardboard man, invisible as the mild air, observing, smiling, anonymous, apart from the big stilted march of gain and loss, violence, speed, defeat. The forsythias crowd about, a cloud of witnesses, every man's forgiveness, a promise kept. I think of the far end of the lane, yearn toward it, in hope it may show the faces of Phil, David, John, some jailed friend (some dead friend—Darst). What might not happen, if one believes?

I want to do an unfashionable thing, in a time which

1

is not so much fashionable—as simply mad. So mad that it has become a wearying stereotype to speak of its madness. Since the admission hangs choking on the air, is part of the daily burden. You young resisters, what of the madness to which we have delivered you, like a sour ration at the cell door? You fervent apostles of war normalcy, you hunted Panthers, you police, you political big-stick wielders, you few men and women faithful to suffering and the long haul, you, my friends, concocting ways of keeping me uncaged, you students pondering a future in the shadow of Dame Liberty violated (your future closing like a vise). For all of you; resisting, resisting resistance, keeping it heated, keeping it cool, you great self-spawning disease, you nation, you of the nation within the nation, still unrecognized, still in bondage—for you. Something unfashionable; one man's spiritual journey. The delayed journey, into light; or more exactly into a light forever quenched, delayed, snuffed out.

To offer a proposition: the state of resistance as a state of life itself. Since like it or not, this is the shape of things. We will not again know sweet normalcy in our lifetime. What seems *outré* now, outrageous, disruptive of routine and pattern, is simply the obscure shape of things unknown, as far as we can discern any shape at all. (We can.) Shapes we can no longer cringe from, run from (very far), bribe out of sight (for very long). All of which, it seems to me, once the admission is made, clears the air. When the future need no longer be resisted, the true form of resistance can be spread out before us, analyzed, dealt, losing hands and winning. All to the good. It being pernicious and lethal and against the right order of things that we should cling to the past, sanctify what we have known, give our hearts to it, sell our souls. No.

Everything begins with that no, spoken with the heart's full energies, a suffering and prophetic word, a word issuing from the nature and direction of things. No. A time to tear and pull down and root out. A time for burning out the accumulated debris of history, the dark noisome corners of our shrines, a universal spring-cleaning. So that the symbolism of Catonsville may become a permanent method and symbol. Of what?

Of moral process. Not of escalated ethical improvement, or social engineering of American dreams, or exportation of techniques. We have had enough of that; we must speak of something other, closer to the dark roots of our existence, to beginnings, to the heart of things.

The Bible has many powerful images to bring reality to our shocked attention once more. Exodus, metanoia, conversion, a new way for man. The mysterious, stormy, jealous, destructive, heartbreaking Other keeps probing the rotten fabric of human invention and arrangement. He will not indefinitely allow man the sweet slavery into which he sinks like a flaccid complaisant lover. No, every slavery is an invitation to another exodus; every exodus is guided by a dark promise. In the course of journeying and hunger and thirst and sin, the tribe comes upon its identity by a singular act of grace. The rites are performed during a pause on the march; they are bloody and primitive, and exact communal and personal remorse, and win forgiveness. Amnesia, forgetfulness, distraction, the lost

3

way, are repaired—by a mysterious choice, by man's choosing to be chosen. The journey continues once more, toward the promise, and its land. And always, by implication, the promise is hedged about with the unknown, the human quantum. Every promise of God continues unkept; the promised land is only one stage of things, infected with the threat of human betrayal. Will systems again captivate man—a new rhetoric, masking the old injustice, lead man to a new enslavement?

I wanted to do something foolish, in a bad time. Those students and resisters and priests and nuns (and blacks and chicanos) who perhaps rejoiced and understood what I had done in going underground—I want above all to avoid offering merely a new kind of captivity, a stasis, food for romantic fascination with what I had done. I want to help others come over into freedom, in the very effort to free myself. I want to suggest a strong note of reserve, of pessimism, of the ambiguous which it seems to me are of the very nature of life today. (Not so much to introduce these qualities, as though from outside, but to point to them as already there, part of the makeup of this, or indeed of any such course of responsible action.) And then to ask: In spite of all, what are we to do with our lives? A question which seems to me a peerless source of freedom to the one who dares pose it with seriousness.

It seems clear by now; anything short of confronting this question ends up sooner or later in a suffocating dead end. We have had a history in recent years, both in the movement and in its expression in the Church, of the inadequacy and emptiness of just such short cuts. We have taken up, one after another, almost every question except the one which would liberate us: the question of man. How is a man to live today? How is he to live; is it possible for a man to do something other than kill his brother—the practically universal demand laid upon him by the state, approved by a silent Church? Is there another way, which will allow men to live here and now; will allow the unborn to get born, and to live their lives in a way different from the (one) way sanctioned today?

Now such a question is first of all a question for the one who poses it. It issues from his mouth, from his life, from his profession, from his family—seriously or frivolously. In the nature of things, the question touches only secondarily on the murderous realities of public policy, consumerism, bribes, duplicity, warmongering, distemper, hell's spiderworks spun across the world, anchored in every place of power. The question (one way of putting the question) is an effort to get at the enslaved unexamined conscience, the lives of those of us not yet grown conscious, the way in which the filament sticks to us and we to it (part of us caught, part free) so that we are in effect mortised into the network, our presence there an enticement and bribe to others.

How shall we live our lives today? It is scarcely possible, it will be less and and less possible, to live them at the center of the web, without being cursed in our humanity, metamorphosed finally into the beast whose activity we take up as our own. The beast who eats men.

It seems to me that two eventualities are in the air, and one of the two will certainly occur, as a fact of history—

and soon. Americans, a certain number of them, will struggle to keep alive a human style and method, to enhance it, rejoice in it, celebrate it; and in so doing, will make it possible for men to be born of men. Or a genetic (which is to say spiritual) catastrophe will occur. The method of the beast will prevail, and beasts will be born of us. I do not know of a more truthful way of putting the question, our destiny, what is to become of us.

Shunting from city to city, dependent on the goodness and ingenuity and risk of a few friends, one comes to a better sense of these things. How are we to live our lives today? We are in the dark preliminary stages of a new humanity, together. Imagine! my brother in prison, myself on the run, our friends here and there (in prison, on the run), and in every city between. Thus, all of us are enabled, in an utterly new way, to probe and ponder the new forms of community, the questions about the future, the usefulness and joy and hope that may arise from this. From physical stasis, and from a slippery, even absurd mobility (in prison, underground)—in both conditions, to explore our spiritual freedom. Am I suffering delusions, or can others see with me the stunning opportunity that opens like a grace before us?

To pose the questions I have suggested, to do it in circumstances which push the questions hard and fast, refusing answers, refusing delay, refusing short circuits and cuts, and temporizing and abstractions and cowardice and amnesia; refusing refusals. Since the times are dark and uncertain (I will be going to jail, as sure as tomorrow. It is as though a man were to awaken one morning with the bitter revelation on his tongue—I am going to die. I am going to jail. Like a man with terminal illness whose cunning apothecary has come on a new potion, I am spared a few days. The days are here. But I live under proviso. That is my freedom and my urgency).

Meantime, I would like to do something unfashionable, in the sense not of mystification, but facing the fact that everything or nearly everything of worth today is despised or devalued.

Except to a few, to whom these words, in all seriousness and affection, are dedicated.

I should like to raise the questions whose very posing implies one is not seeking a more bearable form of insanity or illness in the Imperial Madhouse. One is seeking sanity and health; which is to say, one is at least initially and in principle, on a subversive errand, determined with whatever energy and courage he can summon, to persevere in it. For the rest, let us see.

I should like to use, as a general guide, master text, source of imagery, the book of John of the Cross, *The Dark Night of the Soul*.

The choice is deliberate. It implies in the first place that my present situation is primarily an experience in and of the spirit, that its only coherence and meaning are to be sought on those terms. Otherwise, one is playing cat-and-mouse with the hunters, and the chase becomes frivolous, thoughtless or pathetic, played out according to their feints and starts, exercised in their fears. It should be clear by now perhaps that I am something other than a rodent scurrying about in the labyrinth of power, pro-

7

grammed to stimulus and response. No. I claim for myself the dignity of a Christian and a man, present to his tradition (as chief strength), often faithless to that tradition (as weakness). But in any case, within it; for good, for ill, but unrecognizable to myself apart from it. To be drawn on here and now, quickly, because the times are rude and descend like a guillotine. This saint, John; why him?

He was a resister and prisoner, and suffered grievously, as it happened in the circumstance of his time, at the hands of the Church. No matter; let us say from irrational and inhuman power, in those times (as in our own, in less spectacular ways) wielded by Church as well as state. He was neglected, cast down from the places his talents would justly claim, maligned, broken. Yet in the dark socket of existence into which he had been flung to be ground to powder, a most stunning event occurred. It was as though out of season on the desolate streets near this house, winter-ridden and sullen, a wand of forsythias had burst into bloom, only one. In a dungeon, the light broke upon him. John was granted something due no mortal man: access to the mystery of love, sight of the bare bones and plan of the universe, odor of the heart of Dante's rose.

He wrote an ecstatic poem (poetry—the primary inevitable response to tyranny). Later, in a rare calm interval of his life, he used the poem as source of a prose commentary, which would enlarge and make available, as far as words could, the generous grace and access which had been granted him. Both commentary and poem are among the

8

supreme achievements of the spirit of man: they are open to the reader, the student, the activist, immediate and rich access to the classics of Hindu and Zen. The poem, the commentary; they are all poetry; they improvise with infinite subtlety and unfailing symmetry on a few simple unkillable themes of the spirit. How is one to grow, in love, in the risks of love? What is the price of love? Who is this loving, invading, tireless, mysterious God, whose urgent heart is the very heart of the universe?—who calls out to man, who is silent, silent before omnipresent, omnivorous evil?

Let us move closer to the matter at hand. John is useful to us for such reasons. He suffered greatly, as a condition of life and a condition of faith. He suffered because his convictions were unacceptable to power, ran counter to the grain. He never submitted obediently to Byzantine men, even though their power was announced in awesome rhetoric, and wielded the keys of the divine will. John was seeking a simple human good (we would say today). He wanted a community in which men would choose for themselves how they would live and where, within the freedom granted them by the truth of a tradition.

He was willing to negotiate with opponents; he traveled unwearyingly in service to rational solutions. But when power breathed close and threatened hard, his adversaries came up against something harder than Spanish bone. They struck flint; and flint, in the nature of things, awakened fire. John burned with a fire which human conflict ignited, sustained elsewhere, burning on behalf of men.

Elsewhere? The movement today, in its best parts, in its finest idealism, in those occasions when it is politically most attuned, has always breathed a sense of the transcendent which puts to shame the flat-footed sterile rhetoric and method of current power. The Port Huron statement is a case in point. It is bathed in primitive and tender light; it bespeaks the best in the American grain, as though selective memory and choice (love is always selective) had been able to ignore, to surmount, to treat as of no account, the pervasive horror and violence of American history. New men are appealed to, under the very sign and hypothesis of their newness; an act of creation. Hayden, Oglesby and the others—what a gift they gave us! Was it the innocence that precedes experience, a simple ignorance; or was it an inclusive transcendence? We must hear from these friends again, as indeed we shall . . .

John was known as *"Doctor de la Nada"*; guru of the absurd. It is a title both just and exact, conferred after the fact on a man whose life stood at the heart of darkness.

Are we then merely to seize on the phrase, and by implication on his life, as another loose-jointed excuse for personal adventuring, rootlessness, irresponsibility toward those near and far?

No. John opened before us another way, a precious and neglected truth; the inescapable paradoxes, the burning dialectic of truth; the high-wire act required of the mind that would be—not in possession of, but possessed by—the truth; in passage, and in danger.

An intense passivity, the shaping of man into a receptacle for the light and rain of heaven. If he was Promethean, a world shaper in the justest sense of that word, he not only stole fire. He fulfilled that other, less scrutinized episode of the myth: he was chained to rocks, his vitals were eaten by predators. (Reality is predatory; it not merely presses upon man with the urgency of its evidences, it eats one alive.)

The need of activists, of the best of youth today, is a spiritual need, often expressed to me, often neglected of fulfillment. It is the presence of masters of the spirit, to help them discern what is really happening to their lives, to the forces erupting in their souls. What we used to call the presence of spiritual fathers, to aid in the discernment of spirits. So that the mere surface of things, the shrinking vocabulary, the wounds suffered day after day in the struggle to remain human and to vindicate life, the canker and spur and itch toward violence (in response to entrenched, vapid self-confident violence) so that these can be confronted on other terms than those of spasmodic despair, hit and run, explosion and self-destruction. (Do some activists in such times as these see themselves as little more than self-destroying machines, and so wire their bodies and walk about, pure instruments of terror, like the Anarchist in Conrad, or the prerevolutionary bands of students in Russia?)

I suggest (indeed it was the equivalent method of John), let the monks cut loose from their good order and country discipline and begin with all of us, to make connections anew. Let the communities who have carved on the keystone of their monasteries PAX learn what some of us have paid dearly and known for long: There's a war on; can you

11

smell death? Do you know what peacemaking is costing us? Where are all those good things you purportedly hold in escrow and never share with us? Have you ever attended one of our political trials, seen us dragged off, read the cheap price put on our lives and deaths by the frosty eye of power? I have a dream: I dream of every resisting commune with a guru (Christian, Jewish, Hindu, Zen) in roving residence; sharing that thing, whatever its risks and follies; leading men and women into their unexplored inner spaces; making room for love, for hope, where there seemed no room because there was no light.

Brother David, Mount Saviour, do you read this?

But *"Doctor de la Nada"*—I should like to tell you why that title appears to me to be both delicious and apt. It is from one point of view a way of admitting to ourselves the presence of those dark forces, only partially under our (or anyone's) control; but whose existence, faced in truth, amounts to a kind of exorcism. Since to be hidden and unadmitted to high noon and its scrutiny is their method and source of power. Respectability, morality, abstraction, the flattening out of man, to his assimilation to his artifacts and weaponry.

Doctor de la Nada. One is guru of the absurd or disciple of the guru, under the hypothesis that God is Lord of the Absurd. Touché. The saint has come upon God (and we come upon the saint) not as solution, goal of effort, lover of neatness, scorekeeper of fair games, suburban owner, or any of those "final solutions" which ring down the curtain on reality. No, the saint is going to let the truth out, which is to say let the beasts out, those human beasts with the masks of their choices glued to their faces. And see what happens. And see what one chooses. And go from there.

Do you sense the way of freedom this implies? Note for a moment the contrary method in public vogue. It is curiously, even boringly consistent in vocabulary and form. In virtue of an inherited gentleman's agreement, the power gets passed on, the admissions to the club are laid down. From the UN to the White House to the courts and Congress and Cabinet, the same straight-faced deception rides. Puritan virtue, sternness (only rarely a Reagan; if it must be, let's have the blood bath now), a Hoffman, an Agnew—men who ought to be precious to all of us for letting the truth out of the dark bag, at least now and then. But by and large, straight cut, straight jib. The deeper and bloodier the mess, the straighter, squarer, firmer the stance.

Doctor de la Nada. Even the Church had to swallow it, absurdity at the heart of holiness, at the heart of inspiration and intuition. At the heart of God also? It must be said. Yes. John was setting up a balancing act, upping the ante, opening the door (it was open anyway) on the beasts, all of them: the arts, the atom, space, atheism, technology, grace and damnation, creation, annihilation. How to say it? He was generating a storm, predicting it, welcoming it; the very condition of our lives.

Could this work (the liberating of *Nada* to wrestle with the *All*) be a work of God? Yes, it was.

I want to be faithful to his method, which is rational and coherent, but whose content is also, and from another

13

point of view, surreal, nightmarish. A classicist, an ecstatic, a good fighter, a faithful man, a hound nervous as
lightning in the traces, a merciless surgeon of the soul, a
Jesus prayer.

By Night I Went Out by the Back Window While the FBI Was Fumbling at the Front Door.

By night.

You must find a time when your options are increased, and theirs, at least for a time, diminished. There could be many "you"; you could already have flown the coop—how many windows in how many rooms of an apartment are there? They probably haven't done their homework that well. You have a start.

Moreover, who and where are your friends, what part have they had in this, what forked roads, deceptions, disguises, directions, hidden places, have they come up with? FBHoover doesn't have the slightest.

Moreover, in a community dominated by young people,

who have their own alleys, stairwells, codes, meeting places, language, short cuts, etc., it's hard to get info, unless you're trusted. FBH isn't; you and I are.

Moreover, he's mechanized out of his mind. We saw it in Vietnam; we landed there as though on the moon; technique and garbage fore and aft. And that was supposed to win.

Moreover, the subaltern of power, and the poltroons themselves, were about as familiar with that rich and noble culture (besides which ours is still in dirty disposable d's.), as they are say, with you and me. An enormous advantage, which has been seized on with utmost skill by the people of Vietnamese villages and the vanishing fighters.

How expensive a thing it is to do an unhistorical thing, how clumsy and inevitably bloodletting—for both sides. The war (and this is to our point, as I hope to show) was as impossible as Humpty Dumpty's mythical leap. It was a disaster born, against laws as self-evident as that which Mr. Egg violated. I.e., in our case, you cannot dam up history and its forces indefinitely, and not cook up a major disaster; occurring to yourself. This is consolation too, though a sorry one, for us; caught behind the lines where history is forbidden to happen, desperately trying to help it happen. What could be harder? But at the same time, what more correct, a stunning form of realism?

I want to get back to our night image. And the image of departure. It is indeed a long night for most of us. We had had the naïve well-nurtured idea, some of us, as far back as '63, that the war could be contained; then that it could be turned around; then that new political leadership was the answer; then that the pace and numbers of dissenters should be speeded up in national demonstrations; then that moral and personal witness would light up the night; then that symptoms solely were being dealt with (we must step back and see the disease whole, of which Vietnam was only a tick on the rhino's hide); then that the weather was indeed polluted and sour, and the Weathermen must bring on a storm fast and hard; then dynamiting; then Chicago; then trials, indictments, more trials; then here and there another phenomenon, unnoticed first, then deliberately localized and ignored in the media; the attacks on draft boards . . . then Vietnamization (i.e., expansion; the rule being when the mandarins speak, look for the real move up the sleeve, not in hand or mouth); then, then, then . . .

I am speaking of a long night.

For most SDS, hippies, yippies, Panthers, drug freaks, resisters—for a whole generation—there has been nothing else but the night: the war. Their sensibility has taken shape and misshape in its lurid light, its festering and feverish climate. Darkness, obscenity, nightmare, jeopardy, nausea, despair, stasis, dropout, drugs. Time has gone like a nightmare snake dance, anonymous, without purpose, pure horror, men hidden under the cloth painted like a serpent, the dream that seeks and consumes, wounds and goes free . . .

How build a life worthy of human beings in the darkness? We are called to grow new organs, by new conditions of life and death. New ways of perceiving, of living in the

17

world, new ways of moving over, to give room for others to live at our side. And all without even seeing their faces . . .

Margaret Mead says a great deal. The American family is a perfect nest of sitting ducks for the American Enterprise, that death-ridden domestic and universal plan of non-values and specious control. Produce, in isolation and selfishness, the children who will, as the only available option for human beings, have bought the bag. Thus ensure the ethos and its durability, biologically. Teach the young to grab, to want, to consume, as the first native human gesture. Self-improvement, self-help, consumerism—war: the dregs of the American dream. Silence any other stirrings by conferring a baptismal epithet on them; they are "silent," i.e., they know no other fate, simply because they are forbidden knowledge of any other. They are the "majority," i.e., they are historically irresistible; at home before a nagging, troublesome, but controllable ragtag of malcontents. Irresistible before the world, since power is the last word, and the clout belongs by every point of possession and inheritance to us.

In the midst of this vast machinery of control, install here and there silencers, safety valves, leeway to left and right; build delays, appeals, court liturgies into the law. Fix attention on these, make it all make sense; make it seem generous and humane.

Make of crime and punishment one inseparable process. At the same time, separate lawbreaking from moral intent, forbid legal scrutiny to rest upon the second, in order to concentrate solely on the first. Thus up the ante on illegal dissent, to the point where its punishment makes it an unbearable option to normally good men. Segregate, isolate the lawbreakers from citizenship; prison, exile, the edge.

Keep the "majority" from their earliest years narcoticized with illusions of the good life, security, conventional morality. Do not put the price of the good life too high (but still not too low). Keep them in debt, keep the reminders going, the installments due for payment on deferments of foreclosure—so the future belongs to power, which knows when to play out the line, and when to land the catch.

> On a dark night (John says)
> I went out unseen
> From my house that was at last, at rest.

A remarkably consistent image of historic renewal. "God let the people out, through the wilderness of the Red Sea; the sons of Israel went out of the land of Egypt."

Even where there is no journey out of slavery, perhaps the image is vindicated. Men must cast off their yoke and claim what is theirs; the ground they stand on, the rights violated by unjust aggressors. The life and death of Che and Camilo Torres are an exodus of the spirit no less striking. The exodus and return of Ho, to lead his people "out," the unfinished revolution, his own death seen as the merest momentary interruption—the burden taken up by others; millennial patience, based on unassailable claims to life and freedom, buttressed by courage and hope.

On a dark night
I went out unseen . . .

The longest journey begins with that single step. That
single step, taken by Americans. I have no least doubt as
to the truth of the matter. Nothing will change, seriously,
in the great world, unless we submit to change. What is
the next step?

Not to deny; the Cubans, especially the Vietnamese,
have jammed the wheels of power with enormous effect,
all but upset that obscene chariot and its lethal rake's
progress. But such a tribute to them cannot be made the
occasion of a dodge on our part. What health is there
in our lives, as antibiotic to national raging illness? What
new directions has life assumed, as symbol and substance
of the hope that even Americans may yet evolve into the
human family?

New forms of humane power begin with (1) the renunciation of corrupting, consuming, historically used,
misused, used-up power. This, and (2) the acceptance of
powerlessness (for a time).

The symbol: a going forth, from a house at rest, at
night.

The house: in many senses; the *alma domus*, the struc-
tured universe, womb, rest, tomb; premature age, reward
after effort, retirement plan; or conversely, in a twisted
ancestral sense, family expectation embodied again, Ad-
am's values in Cain. Taboos observed, conventional morality. And accomplishments, enhancements, the extension
of family demesnes; Eden, its spoilage reclaimed, its ten-

ants pacified. Sense of the world, and time; abstraction, remoteness from the funk, fury, mire of actual life. The Brooks-suited investor, consumer, power player, infinitely removed from the bloodletting his manicured fingers set in motion. Language; politesse, a genius at fulfilling in national and local circles the expectations of other beneficent (and benefiting) buccaneers—the shareholders, the homeowners; triviality, stereotypes, heartlessness, deception, as methods of power.

Are the sons to inhabit the house, shore up its walls, tend its gardens, preserve and enhance its specious honor?

Or are they to "go out?"

The time is here (is at hand) when middle America will choose between its property and its sons. Is at hand. And the choice, when the chips are down, is already made: the renunciation of the bloodline in favor of possessions. Helicopters over Berkeley, Weathermen hunted down, resisters in jail or exile. Case of one resister: his father sat stonily on the draft board which rejected his plea for a CO. The father urged in fact, secretly, the severest prosecution of his son . . .

To go out from such homes, such fathers, such values, is no great task. How many sons and daughters, from early adolescence, burn with secret hatred and despair, for having to sit day after day at such tables, submit before such opinions, attend such schools and churches, accept such money, bear such resemblances in features, voice. Strangers in a strange land. Sanity itself begins with estrangement—from madness.

The question is obviously not one of merely going out,

as into a void. The question is one of alternatives; a second sight in the darkness, cat's eyes—or panther's. But a deep draught of gall from a cup held by some parent's hand, is often the stirrup cup of the future; such bitter ingredients of (so-called) life.

The tension is heightened when the university attempts further to legitimate tribal arrangements. But neither home nor university has been able to prevent or even seriously to inhibit, what goes on at the edges of each, under the nose and eyes of legitimacy. And what goes on there is precisely the undermining of both; the struggle is pushed further, into earlier consciousness, all the time. It is a portent, capable of the most serious political application, and consequence.

> Went out, my house
> being at peace.

I find the image vastly puzzling and intriguing. Whose house is at peace today? And if at peace, why the walk out? Isn't it simple good sense, if one has gotten that peace in
> hand, to hang
> > around and enjoy it, foster it, impregnate others with
> > it?
Yet how about this?—midnight (says the poem)
> the furniture breathing in its place, the cat curled
> up like a pacified universe
momma and poppa bedded down in their sexual tomb
the electric eyes glowing like Dobermans, waiting the first
> hypothetic move of

the first hypothetical thief, there in alley or hedge
Pure American! pure deception! sons and daughters
those straight clean bodies, those straight clean minds
blank as bed sheets *tabula rasa* dreaming the tribal dreams
       Yes.
tomorrow   the big dip in the big cultural vat   children
    like flags
      red   white   blue   minds   bodies
O those altitudinous lives   swung upward
     faster than children or alpiners
      captive voluminously free   ropes and metals
      the clanking halyards
Say can you see!   the eyes of one third of the world
      developed eyes   schooled eyes   legal eyes   cher-
      ished eyes
      swing upward after   O guerdon and emblem   so
      proudly we hail!

No, it is a question of a false peace, maintained by terror
persuaded day in and out, by every device of deception, of
its own rights and privileges, as inalienable, inherited, right
and just. So that the fate of the majority of men (How
desperately the rich need the poor—create the poor) is
placed off at the edge of the eye, never at dead center; is
thus relegated to the status of minor annoyance, minor
offense, like cancer, smoke fumes, subway delays, the mal-
functioning of an old man's heart. Somewhere, the misery
of the majority; physically quite near, pressing upon us
with its evidence—but rendered remote as say, the roped
bodies floating down the Mekong, swollen, face down.

An extraordinary achievement! guns paid for, soldiers trained by US authority, crossed a border, rounded up these men and women, executed them, flung them in the river by the hundreds. The facts are reported in the American press. What is of interest (the thing has happened many times before, the evidence is always in, it is one of the glories of a "free press"; maintained because it is in practice harmless; men see and take no action, eyes are blind as putty); how men can be isolated by a synthesis of fear, hatred, indifference and selfishness. So that the retention of privilege (the guns, the teeth of the Doberman) is at center eye, center brain; and actual starvation, waste, looting, murder, violation, exiling, political domination of others, is reduced to the moral value of a myth, the obsession of a minority of troublemakers and misfits.

Whose house is at peace, what sort of peace?

I want to admit as altogether crucial ingredients of such peace (genuine peace), anger, frustration, despair, disgust, disillusion, dread. I speak of the peace that has sucked up, transfigured, assimilated all these reactions to idiocy and public horror. A man is of no use to the future unless the full force of the present world has turned him inside out, like a pocket before a mugger and his knife. Stripped clean!

Stripped clean I wish to say, so that a man joins, at one liberating stroke, the masses who have also been stripped clean by the mugger, the exploiter, the respectable thief. And being so violated, and understanding the simultaneous and systematic violation of their brothers throughout the world, have passed into new ways of thought, new ways of living, have seen themselves in a totally new way, neither that of victim (to which the theft aimed at reducing them) nor that of accomplice or thief.

Now we are coming closer, I think. It is this sort of peace, the icy unshakeable resolve of the violated man, unified from heart to guts to fingertips, the poet speaks of. Some great wrong has been done him, some great theft worked on him. His birthright; the decent community, the presence of his brothers, access to humane public structures, a place in building the future? All of these.

What he goes out of, after all, is himself. The house as image. It is the static laid-at-rest supposition, the past that was presumed to have final power over his future. That empowering, possessive myth, the father who laid hold and would not let go.

Let my people go. Alienation, disruption; all forms of violence break out on the enchanted atmosphere. The polis had been at peace, Pharaoh's imperial will shed a light of purest gold on the public undertaking, guaranteed the immortality of all who took part. The web of life shuttled, a clean and classic pattern from birth to grave. In its linen, a chief would be wrapped at birth, its pattern would grace the form of Pharaoh's mummy, emblem and sign of immortality.

Who heard from the slaves, who cared? They were part of the public arrangement, executors of the public will; honored thereby, drawn into an enterprise forever beyond their realizing.

When the slave is a slave, all is well in the commonwealth. The most devoted and religious of men thank their gods for peace.

25

Then, Black power!

Moses murders a guard of public order. All hell is at large.

A slave's revolt.

The gods are involved. They are after all the ultimate custodians of that order. They gave it legitimacy, beyond question, a transcendent blessing upon the status quo. The rites awakened remembrance of that order, codified it, dramatized it, drew believers deeper into its web. The gods spoke; gods of citizenship, of order, of war, of imperialism, of the edges of expanding empire, of domination and power, of colonials.

If such gods did not exist, they were shortly created. They are the idols of men's imagination, the embodiment of their dreams, the realization of empire. On occasion, they were also exported, along with their missioners, to announce the gospel of enslavement to the benighted colonies. One cultural imperial web, stretched tightly over the tent of empire.

What is new, what is strange in our present case, how the sons of the possessors have joined the sons of the slaves, in one vast spasm of revulsion. As though Pharaoh's son had conspired with Moses to bring down the empire. Cleaver saw it happening.

We must also see it happening. The No spoken against national policy is cutting across all old inherited lines. It is a source of enormous self-understanding. Source of the peace that can leave the rotten dwelling, and its deceptive peace, declared at the point of guns and dogs, legitimated in the courts, vindicated and protected by the jails.

26

Leaving the house. It has to do with the beginnings, the first stirrings of conscience, the first serious step as a consequence, the first march, the first legal jeopardy, the first trial attended. And everything serious after; the first trial, as defendant now; in the docks, the new play of relationships, the rupture of old safety devices, the cutting loose. Then too, the decision to refuse to pay the piper. Going underground?

And at peace, all the way, as described above. Carrying along one's whole life with him; the sum of its parts and experiences, the new light, the achieved freedom and integrity.

I well remember how the nine of us stood up in the court some two years ago, straight and in black (we impeccable clerics, knowing what we were about, playing to the hilt a game whose rules dictated the plunging of that weapon into us—to the hilt). Yes, your honor. We did it, sir. Knowing that the only point, the only usefulness of Catonsville would be the forum we could gather about the issues we had tried to raise. Knowing the outcome in our well-articulated, not too prophetic bones. Three years; in the kingdom of bluebottle flies, the eating of flesh is the game.

Now they have the flesh of several of us, death eats the flesh of David Darst. We have been through a great deal since that May day; a great deal, given our culture, given what our skins are presumed able to endure. Not much for a Vietnamese, or a Guatemalan, or a Panther, who drag death about with them, and violence, like their own shadow. But for us, retarded and shielded as we have been from the experience of man, something.

Every new step is, to the last step taken, a leaving of the house. How speak of our decision; that some of us would take the next step, would leave the house of that last decision, a logical next step in the same direction? I was again like a child, the first step in the world still untried, one hand slowly leaving the stick of furniture that held the child up. An act of trust, in reality itself; in friendship, its embodiment. Try it!

I am three weeks at large, to this hour. Last night, the President announced the newest move in the war; a move already taken, to assure the peace. It was a move so predictable, so stereotyped, as to rustle the yellowing pages of the *Times*, ten years old. It was a military move, the single move available to bankrupt power: cross another border, subvert a government, seize an enemy sanctuary.

In the deepest night, the eye of the imagination burns like a tiger's. The billboards today are aflame with new posters: Cambodia, No! but who will translate the imperative into political action. Can my friends and I?

The Dark Night of Resistance, in Which All Antics, Attitudes, Whisperings, and Especially Freedoms and Unfreedoms and Their Mimics and Grimaces, Are Abroad; A Witch's Night, in Short.

Those in power used to carry around with them leather draw sacks, filled with goodies for the constituency.

Here and there, say whenever a TV camera is on the scene, it is a favorite ploy, much beloved of fish wandering around, looking for some relief from postmeridian gas in the great Tank Where No Think is Thought, to have some Leader stand there and take out, one by one, the unrepeatable, fresh-caught pelts, those signs of special social concern for the natives; to hold these up—a coonskin, a scalp of a VC. Doesn't that prove (any fish head can

lip-read) how much Daddy cares? Don't I care more than
any daddy heretofore? So there; only a braying jackass and
his improbable first born would vote me out of your eye,
ear, throat and nose. Huh?

It takes only a small flick of the immaculate wrist to toss
the emblem over the tank wall. The fish can do what they
want (they're free, aren't they) with it; as the hairpiece
streams down through the waters before their filmy, be-
wildered gaze. Now what's he tossed us? Doesn't he know
what we really need is wall-to-wall carpeting in here?
Wasn't that definitely one of the first underscored campaign promises he made? What the hell do we need another
scalp for? The place is littered as a tepee in open season
now; we've got King George's men (redheads), Mohegan
Indians (an oil slick), Mexicans, Sitting Bull, Southerners,
Northerners, rednecks (their black polls), slaves, cotton
kings, lumberjacks, gold rushers, doughboys; there's a heap
of niggers in this yere woodpile. We got a Mississippi card
shark down here; he's got an ace in his hair. We got a
twenty-year run on southeast Asians; little scalps, monkey
wise. 'N so on. How the hell you going to find your braces,
eyeglasses, tabac, walking stick, or sunning raft down here,
all this hair clogging up the place? Galumph galumph.
He looked in, they looked out. He acted as though they
read lips; he knew they didn't know reading lips in front
of fish tanks is strictly a campaign project. You nod and
smile and look wise-assed like a catfish, for the cameras,
for the catfish. It's like visiting the home for the feeble-
minded, really; same timing; or toothless old fool Grandma

at Thanksgiving, it makes a nice label for the next recording of "My Wisdom and Aphorism." So-o-o.

Peerless was standing there one day at the fish tank. He took out from the bottomless bag a demised cat, striped like a salmon, for fishy affinity. Held it up. Now this here cat was dead as the doornail lodged in its dumb skull. But it had died in the Great Struggle. Its teeth and lips still grimaced as though forming once more its last words, like a musical score. Left to right, you could read its Cause, following that ravaged line. FREEDOM NOW was what the notes said. Peerless pawed and stroked the cat, crooning to it, the fish could lip-read the croons.

The fish were drawn up to the glass by now, there was not a political doubter in all the tank. All that brain food, so little brains! Snub-nosed, gargantuan of eye; the bubbles went up in unison. Peerless was stroking away at the cat, as though he could warm it up again, for a few more Last Words. That cat got doornailed for freedom, he was a martyr all right; but I ask you: Who was the father of martyrs? Who blessed and honored dishonored cats, dead cats, dead for freedom? Why Peerless, that was who!

By and by, Peerless finished the fiftieth quatrain of the Oboe Hymn To Be Hummed at the Obsequies of Martyred Cats, One for Each State. He wiped the Cat, Downstroke with an American flag; then, tragically, his own eyes. The flag was then folded liturgically by two marines, and slipped into the cat's breast pocket.

There was a roll of drums. Peerless, whose elbow had been lent skill by tossing the first ball at the National League opener, a week before, tossed the cat to glory. In-

31

side the tank, like missiles on gantries, the fish shifted vertical, mouths open, a long hit in the ball park. The cat flew and flew a Nijinsky-like moment, pure stasis, apotheosis, up there, higher than any cat ever flew, glory, glory, unnailed for freedom. He landed belly first; it wasn't graceful, it was mystical. Freedom Cat's tenth life was under way. The fish followed him down.

Fathers and Sons: Utopian Proposals Scrawled on Cave Walls by Those Who Had Everything to Lose, Whose Hand Therefore Was Steady and Inventive, as in the Light

"Slavery can have no part in freedom; freedom cannot dwell in a heart that is enslaved to this or that. Freedom dwells in the heart of a free man, for his heart is that of a son."

The discussion is about connections and freedom. The two seem to be natural enemies, lined up for a go, spoiling for it. To get disconnected seems to be the first job of all, for now; to make a break from all the enslavements and enticements that rope us cunningly to one another, like prisoners after a search-and-destroy hunt.

33

Follow the rope around the world, the intuition goes. Its naked knot closes around the throat of a dying man, woman, child; whose chief offense is that they put their lives (outrageously, surplus lives anyway) in the path of the Machine. Waste them; the word comes down; Song My is its moment.

It may well be necessary to die, to save one other man, woman or child. The time for that seems near. It may also be necessary to live on, to launch one's self on the desperate, unrewarded long haul. Between Che and A. J. Muste, who is to judge or choose?

The break with false, enslaving connections, cuffs, body chains (at times), parents, churches, schools; the human and institutional breaks—simply to get free, as though one were the first man ever to walk the earth. I do not want to underplay the cruelty, surgical pain of what is sometimes required, as a strict postulate of conscience, existence itself, of young people. The first step toward freedom is the cutting of the umbilical of unfreedom. You do not know what lies beyond. If you do know, you are probably on the wrong track, something remains that is not your due, your life and its plan still lie in someone else's pocket. Who is his own man? Who is, not his father's son, but his father's ape? In bad times, racked by fear, fathers no longer want sons, except in their image, which is to say their stereotype; which is to say, they set about begetting apes. History stops here, with the selfish. (I am not trying to be moralistic, to pass judgment, which today is about as useful as passing feces.) What we are asked to do is merely to attend to the truth of things, out of which morality may be presumed to arise.

34

John of the Cross connects freedom with sonship. But life today seems to demand, time and again, that sons disconnect from their fathers. Is there a truth here, worried about by dilemma, but still extricable? Who can take away, without further wounds, that fierce necessity which binds us, biologically even, even in terror, to that face, those words, that hand laid on our lives? To have reached the truth of that relationship is, now and again, to touch the truth of the world.

In a given culture: the older stable European view, the hold of the tribe on its youth, the stern lessons, by rote, of the language, feasts of memory, mysteries enacted, the creation of a future faithful to the past. Weakness: servility, plodding the old track, the domesticated imagination, moral drift and decay, growing old without having been young.

In our culture; dada, babyhood, the cribbing and confining of virtue to the cribside. A lack of density, cultural richness. The father as salesman; and the death thereof. Mama holding the reins of the team, father and son castrated in service to the goddess and her trivial suburban vision. On the other hand, cultural explosion, uncontained, liberating, propelling the whole enterprise out of its skin and head. Where indeed is our son? in jail? in exile? in the Sierras? on pot? The cast is threepenny opera, pure art, pure horror, pure future. Largest possible cultural exposure, pushed hard and early; travel, easy riding, moving cool, refusing to stoke the fires under the (formerly) hot idols; he pisses on them. The gods crack as they cool.

One difficulty underscores the general undermining of

35

the relationship. The assault on *admiration*. It is practically impossible, given the brute movement of technology into every human relationship, for the son to discern the features of the father. What is he really like anyway, this nine-to-five harassed part-timer, this giver of life gone sour, this creature of so little leisure, compassion, inwardness, wisdom, center?

Almost no son today can see his father against a landscape of human usefulness, celebration, simplicity. Whose father offers anything primitive, spontaneous, either in art or the making or deployment of tools? That might be the question of childhood; as it grows graver, the question cuts deeper. Is he doing something useful, a human gift to humans, with his life? What excitement is there to him; what light is around his body?

Technology, as it has gone the past twenty years, lays a blunt sword between every human relationship. It has no interest, no *telos*, no will to enhance or grace life; it has gone to war; and all its touching of humans is by way of paramilitary damage. Not outrage, as its main military presence works, in brute destruction of the ecology and lives of the East.

But something lethal here, too; inevitably. So the question for sons hangs unanswered, is part of the torture of fathers. What to do with one's life, what human implication survives? And in a culture given over to the uses and para uses of death, triviality, distraction—in domestic and foreign package and brand—how is a man to be a man, before his son, before his marriage, before his community or God? And the son: How is it I can't even *see* him;

what a relief it would be even to be able to hate him. But how do you hate a benign blur?

Practically, in most cases, no clear line can be strung between the eye of a son and the life of his father along which either or both can run. In the way of positive approval, of admiration of a trade, discipline, talent launched, recognized, rightly valued. A few artists, writers, ministers, activists survive; if the father keeps the son's admiration, if the son runs with the father, an ongoing model for the life of conscience—it is invariably because their awakening and level of understanding run parallel. Both are in the same bag. Economics, politics, moral sense; they are linked, in movement. And know they will shortly, if not already, begin to suffer for it.

But paying up is not the skill of the middle class. To most, installment living is not a metaphor, it is a trap. Moral accountability? Such a life as lays hands seriously on the wounds of man, a surgical endeavor that has healed the humane center of that (or any) profession? O that I could see the face of my father!

You begin somewhere. Most sons pick up the thread of the labyrinth in the darkness, follow it blindly, in rage, in tears. That slimy coil is no substitute for a father's hand.

But what if that hand is offered as an amputated thing (not cleanly amputated, torn off) left at one's feet, dropped there by a running dog? The nightmare is a stereotype; most of us connect (if the truth is told) with limbs and shanks and bones of men, rather than with the living. One way of putting the rage of the young: who wants to be fastened to a dead limb?

37

Fathers and sons, in the good or ill estate of that reality, read the times. Today, weep.

Is there a substitute for a lost relationship that will not mark us with a grievous wound?

Grievous, lethal, slight—there is nothing today that does not leave a wound. In the darkness you reach out as you can. The sons of good men are not thereby immune from suffering. Any more than the sons of let us say agents of the CIA. There is no protection in anything—as good parents say ruefully. There is only the perdurance in the young (if their beginnings are fortunate) of the memory of warmth, decency, respect, space to move in, to be freakish in, to be a fool in. Space to be young in. There is some slight evidence that against all the tawdry, nearly universal later evidence of what theology used to call "total corruption," the memory might prevail, the stubbornness of a living thing. Parents live with a stone in their guts, and say to one another, and each to himself, in a rictus of anguish and perplexity, a hundred times a day or night: I do not know. Merciful and compassionate, they attempt to conceal their suffering from one another. But they conceal nothing.

That the Monk and the Activist Ought to Sit Down Together: That Would Indeed Be Something More for Us Than the Usual Tawdry Fancy Footwork of Heads of State or Bodies Politic.

One of the best things I could think of doing before leaving Cornell, was to take out an ad in the U paper, inviting some resisters to a local monastery for a weekend of prayer, song, and discussion. It turned out a mixed blessing, with a great deal to be said for the credit side. Something "generational" was set up and fueled to the lid. The young vs. the elders; faith vs. humanism; flight from the world vs. the big leap. The monks came along to take part, but at most of the sessions remained without voice or vote—by their own choice. You felt the con-

39

trasts in the air; the long-smoldering, patient watch fires of prayer, the candor and gentleness limned into the monks' faces, young and old. And then in the students, the suddenness, flare, instantaneous anger, the flashpan of suspicion, fury, joy, surprise, insight, uncharity, words that cut deep and quick, vulgarisms, intolerance, the gnawing and digging for the truth of things . . . those students, whose childhood had been war, whose youth is war, who have been handed a bill of goods in a chic package, and told, with the leer of the old con man, Go ahead, buy it . . . And then, after repeated refusals to be hooked, the threat: Buy it, kid, or else.

The threat is there, the menace lying in wait. They know it themselves, they know it is true, a fact of existence for others infinitely more constant, menacing, inescapable; for the poor, the Panthers, their peers in everything except experience of life itself.

> It is clear that desires weary and exasperate the soul, for they are like restless and discontented children, who are ever demanding one thing or another from their mother, and are never satisfied.

John of the Cross puts the dilemma. Another way of saying: he solves nothing, he sets up an argument.

It is not merely that he is using language we no longer find helpful (children, mothers, woolly flocks of desires, childishness). Almost any of us would admit today—perhaps even the monks would admit it, in proportion as the cry of youth, its outrage, its lost chance, reach us, them—it is clear that John states only one side of a case, as though it were the whole case. Nothing as complex as the world undoubtedly is, can be so neatly disposed of. It is a monk speaking, and monks, even the holiest, are unerringly absolutist. It is their métier; the divine, the naked edge, eternity, postulates of obedience and submission laid on men; the consequent cloud laid across human enterprise. And finally what the great majority of the young would suspect today, the defamation of man, to the greater honor and glory of God. . . .

Yet the monk has (if he knows what some of us have endured, tried for, failed at) a strong handle against us. Most of the young are ignorant as rain, of the resources faith has so long offered man. This is, from any thoughtful point of view, one of the great unexamined tragedies. Today the universal invitation to transcendence—in work, in art, in prayer, in human love—is so shot through with cultural and political rot that the young turn away in instinctive disgust. That? religion? That kind of god? No thanks.

For them (who after all are presumed to be free and capable of choosing their style and direction), there are only a handful of men and women from whom they would hear such an idea, or hearken to it. A handful of teachers, friends; rarely a parent, most rarely of all, a priest or rabbi. The consequent religious blackout is very nearly complete. Because the revulsion is up close, the figure of one or another betrayer, purveyor, huckster, tends to block out the whole history. They leap to the universal: If these people are so awful, it must all have been like that!

How do you suggest, in such circumstances, the fact of

those brief exceptional lives that stand in every culture and time, very nearly the only justification for the human enterprise at all? who, if the truth were known, stood and stand with every man who seeks his own soul? who across the foul currents of blood and power, said their simple *no*; and often died for it? The absence of saints is among the greatest of losses to the consciousness of a whole culture; one way of putting our disarray. But what of the monks, who believe in saints, hearken to them across death and time, summon their *numen* at Mass, ponder their lives, draw on their example? Good for them, the young might say with irony. A great difficulty is raised. It is a question of translation, of coming across, or not. Of being able to exercise outside the Mass, the main business of the Mass, *Anamnesis*, vital embodied memory, an act on behalf of life, a violent death undergone for orders, a life made available to the living in a daily denial of the supervenient power of death. Does anything like this come across today, from monks and their brothers?

The question has been given an edge by the same forces prowling the world today, which once claimed John, Augustine, Jesus, Isaiah, Buddha, for its own. But the ground has changed under our feet. It is not a question of "charitableness," a "good intention" toward the living, the binding up of wounds, the Sister of Mercy on the battlefield, relief offered plague victims, preaching of crusades. That may have been the question once; it is not the question today. Former methods of mobilizing lives and conscience, certain religious expressions, ways of approaching and symbolizing the divine, easing of the human condition; everyone takes it up anew, a certain eye to the past—but not the center eye. Beyond doubt, the forces operative, against life, against decent community, have universalized, shown their folly and rage and asserted their omnipotence in new ways. Modern power, power politics, have universalized, have seized on man's freedom and integrity, in ways which believers and disciples in the main were not able to grasp.

The difficulty is of course not an abstract one at all, in any real sense. There are few deeper forms of suffering today than that of the monk who senses he is caught as an insider (in "enclosure") with no way out: unless it be the alienation of a student, knowing that to be true to anything human in his makeup, he must face the stigma of being an outsider, with no way in.

It was a troubled, electric forty-eight hours at the monastery, for all concerned. One hesitates to become portentous about it, but it leaves a sense that more than met the eye was in the air in that time and place.

The students, first of all, have no practical confidence in the possibility that other methods of human change are possible than what five short years (their average span of awareness) have been able to accumulate. There is very little mediation between their hands and their books; both of them in a way quite deficient as tools of getting at reality; the one distorting by immediacy, the other by abstraction. One senses so often the cry, in so many corners and turns of their gesture and language, for someone, some presence that is not merely trumpeting the slogans of their ethics or ideology. Some way of coming at the hard nub of the world with a different tool. Some-one to be trusted. Someone else's experience to induce other ways of looking. Silences, hymns, liturgies, relief from the crass buff and rebuff of the problematic, the pin-ball games as universe. More of history immediately avail-able. A broader experience to relieve their own cramped few years, their loneliness, the anguish and anger in the air whenever they gather—the insistence on connections with what is happening to "brothers and sisters."

Even in their anger, there was an acute, quite accurate understanding in the students—of what the monks were, what they had to offer (and were not in fact offering). There was a cry barely audible across a contrary and complaining tone; why can't you be what you might be—(or the ethical push)—what you should be!

All this was beyond doubt annoying to a group of men whose lives are in any case physically hard, who give in not a whit to the comforts and distractions their critics take so for granted: from pot to casual love to endless rapping. But at least part of the trouble was genuine and deep; the monks had been touched; they were being challenged on home ground, in a way they could never have chal-lenged one another—being insiders all, and strictly seg-regated. Even the crowds who came for Sunday Mass from the neighboring town were not to be compared with the students as "opposite numbers." They are, by and large, people whose views are heavily dosed with monastic rose water; they would never expect, one would think, a political sermon from the abbot; a stinging dissection, say, of the latest American idiocy abroad or at home.

No, it was in the course of a weekend such as this, I thought, that the lines could be most clearly drawn and the right questions aired. There could, in fact, hardly be a better occasion, or better people to come together to have things out. Both sides could go far beyond the faddists of "sensitivity" play acting, social engineering, politesse and mindless courtesies that so often bring Americans face to face today, the leaders of a lemming festival. Together for what, for whom? No, both monks and students are serious in ways very few can match; about life, about mystery and human break-through, about crisis and the formation of new men. The monks bring heavy luggage and good credentials; even the worst of societies, before it goes entirely under, is willing to pay a grudging tribute to their goodness, and allow them to exist. But the best thing about them is their perdurance in bad and good times (both, almost bound to be bad times; as cold war is real war). They are like Pharaoh's wheat; we need to know there were men, millennia ago, who ate bread; here it is, whole wheat, whole men in germ.

"Then for Christ's sake, let's make bread!" shout the students. And of course they are right too. People *are* starving (the monks might say, and with some reason; we are too. Their diet was not much more than an edgy concession to keep the extremities warm). But the point, as both monk and student know: there is a great dignity in being able to choose to eat very little, instead of being flung like a dying animal, at birth, onto a compost heap where quick death is a blessing and survival a curse.

Well, I thank the students and I thank the monks, and

I hope they have the grace now and again, in their thoughts, to thank one another, I being absent. Thanks for what? For realizing, in however dim a way, that the death of man occurs when he shuts his door on a strange face. In this case the students, hard-nosed, born out of different-colored eggs in distant nests, fed a different diet of information and value, raised in different climates; examples finally of that precious, precarious, nearly disastrous thing called human variety. Whose definitive extinction (given some chance idiot in power, who controls as he befouls the nest), we call war. To the point even that we can accept this, peace today is so assailed, our minds so weighted by its horrors, that peace will have, at first gaze, some of the same smell of sulphur on it, as war itself. We can hardly get together today, even under the noblest auspices, without shortly being at one another's throat. Peace at length, or more war? It is hard beyond telling, that enduring patience should so seldom be come by, so often defaulted, even by the best men. Our brains being worn to exasperation, and signs of welcome and acceptance being so hard to raise; the winds being so contrary, spiteful.

Older movement people ask (and they are right): How is it there are so few signs of affection among you today?

The monks might have asked the same things. The itch to be at one another's throat is so constant, so destructive; our Peerless Leaders must say to themselves with occasional satisfaction: Leave them alone; they'll pull one another to pieces; who needs us?

But the heat of the questions is a good sign too. It is

the fever of both death and birth that afflicts us. There is no point in thinking that men and women can operate out of cool verbal assumptions, or that rationalism, sanity, clear thought, etc., are going to carry the day, as working assumptions, or neutral points of contact. The gesture that counts, today, is not the word at all; as though sentences, written or spoken, conveyed only the burden of their words. No, there are hidden meanings everywhere, only a fool refuses to read them; from the latest war pronouncement justifying the latest atrocity, to the reading of the Gospel by a monk from the altar. Thoughtful men neither rejoice nor mourn too quickly; they sit there or stand there, and wait for the clues—with the nagging sense, peculiar to experience, that any news is bound to be bad.

But where does one's life stand? That the question is put at all to monks is a kind of crude graffito tribute, distain or mockery, no matter. The point is, who would bother putting such a question to a general or a president—or even in most cases, to one's own parent? One comes to expect the worst; it is almost the sum of one's life, deception, trickery, misuse. Still, maybe, maybe in one or two cases—? The students are looking (almost all of us are looking) for ways to be private men. Modern life has cast us out, without pelt or plumage, into the exterior darkness, wailing and gnashing of teeth. What might it be in such a time to have a center, a nest, an inner space? How would one foster it, share it, make it a communitarian ideal? What has transcendence to do with being a man, secularized, scrubbed clean as an old bone of mystery,

47

dance, joy, free movement, hope itself? (They suspect it has everything to do with it, everything to do with waging a better fight, lasting longer.)

And can a sense of the "other side," inwardness, distance, be fostered without copping out? It seems often (always?) that cultural methods of revolution, new styles in music, dance, the rhythms that rise out of politics, American history, family, regionalism, etc., are only another turn of the squirrel cage. It goes faster, it is electric, fascinating, but who could call it freedom? There is a great measure of health in the monk's daily stint of work and worship. What of the health their work instills? It must be praised and attended to. At the same time, criticism is also in order; what if the same effort were to go into urban work, what if a part of the community lived among the urban poor, shared their skills there, invited students to join them in setting up work communes? Suppose mobile teams of monks, using the monastery as their home base, followed the trail of migrant workers, joining them in planting and harvesting? Because they were technically adept and so had some clout, the monks could defend the workers, help effective organization get going, in what must surely be one of the most inhuman work situations anywhere in the country.

Indeed all forms of life are assaulted by the most ominous implications. The monks suspect it, to their unease; the students know it, to their wrath. To live as a man is to face the whirlwind. More. To live consciously is to sow the whirlwind. Supposing it means something to go on somehow, how much seed reaches the furrow, how much is lost and scattered in the storm? We have the darkest forebodings—and we are right. Any student knows, to be a student, to be faithful to others, to expose the deep illness of university structure, to speak up on the war—is to be under the gun. Americans are dying for these things. Which is simply to say: we are joining the chancy fate of most men, in most of the world, as that fate is decreed by American power and method.

And what about the monks? Can they survive? Would they make it, as a community, if they were to scatter in small groups, take public jobs, take on team responsibilities, break out of the corral? There is no big prevailing evidence it would work, for very long, that they could take the heat, could find ways of worship, new insights, the patience needed to turn such corners.

Still, something favors such a try. Granted certain suppositions of the Gospel, certain unfulfilled needs of men and women, ours may be a moment, not for weighing of logic and good sense against risky waters. It may be time to go ahead, the chances being large that one will die in the effort, or go down, or achieve nothing. But how else will we get out of our corner, into which we are more feverishly painting ourselves? Pharaoh's wheat must die, or to all practical intent, it remains dead as Pharaoh. Such a truth, the students have come on. Their rage is right.

Certain Occult Utterances from the Under Ground and Its Guardian Sphinx

If you seek pleasure in everything
you must seek pleasure in nothing

if you wish to possess everything
you must desire to possess nothing

if you wish to become all
you must desire to be nothing

if you wish to know all
you must desire to know nothing

if you wish to arrive where you know not
you must go by a way you know not

if you wish to possess what you do not
you must dispossess

if you wish to become a new man
you must become a dead man

Koan and Commentary on the Preceding

Disciple: How do I attain ultimate reality?
Master: It is May. Seek a tulip in hell, and bring it back.

Disciple: Today is the feast of the full moon. What is a
       suitable religious gesture?
Master: Obtain a flag of the nation. Obtain a plastic
       image of Jesus. Wrap the second in the first. Offer
       it decent burial in the courtyard.

The master went walking in a wood. His senses were
drawn to a flowering lilac. He thought first: I will pluck a
garland, bear it home, place it in a vase, for rejoicing in the
new season. His second thought was: No, I will breathe it,
and remember. His third thought: I will do neither. He
passed by.

Youth: How do I attain perfect freedom?
Friend: By the way of imperfect freedom. Resist.
Youth: But how?
Friend: Bear with yourself and the world. For one day.

When the way was smooth, the Buddha walked it. When it was rough, he rested frequently. When he was hungry, he ate. When weary, he slept. Thus he attained perfection.

Jesus said: If your eye is a scandal to you, pluck it out. If your right hand offends you, cut it off. This was a hard saying, and many turned back. The wisdom of the masters was made for difficult times, as well as easy. Many sought out the master and said: I do not understand. Tyranny and treason are abroad, good men go under. What am I to do? To all of which complaints and questions, he answered not a word. But if one came and sat before him in silence, the master would bestir himself and speak.

The way, it is said, is the way. You must not hinder the arrow in flight, nor the turtle in his steady pace.

Various cries were raised, standards and placards were fashioned, tumult was raised in the street. Above the clamor, the monks could be heard chanting: If you wish to become a new man, become a dead man.

Disciple: Please tell me of the ultimate truth.
Master: (In a rare gesture, reaching out his hand.) Give me your hand.

Again: Master, I would be non-violent in every thought and deed. Please instruct me in this. But the master grasped his bamboo stick, and struck the disciple with all his strength across the shoulders.

53

Jesus said: Whoever saves his life shall lose it; and whoever loses his life for my sake, will save it.

He said: When you pray, use somewhat these words. Our father who are in the world and surpass the world. Blessed be your presence, in us, in animals and flowers, in still air and winds. May justice and peace dwell among us, as you come to us. Your will be our will; your will that we be brothers, as bread is bread, water is itself; for our hunger, for quenching of thirst. Forgive us. We walk crookedly in the world, are perverse, and fail of our promise. But we would be men, if only you consent to stir up our hearts. Amen.

Job prayed: If I have eaten of my morsel alone, and the fatherless have not shared in it, let my arm fall from its shoulder.

Proverbs: As coals are to burning coals, and wood to fire; so is a contentious man to kindle strife.

Tao: Mistrust of the human intervention which clogs the channels of the Way.

In the darkness of the master's room, the young man talked on and on. Mostly grievance, mostly just. Nation rising against nation, famines, pestilences, earthquakes, men delivered up to be afflicted and put to death, many betrayed and hated for the sake of the truth. False prophets and deceivers abroad, good men turned aside. It was said also that in certain places the sun was darkened, the moon gave no light, the stars fell from the sky. Two men were in the fields, master; one was taken and the other left. Two women were grinding at the mill; one was taken and the other left. And what am I to do; he gestured feverishly in the fading light. I am conscripted for evil, I must kill or refuse to kill; and the price of refusal is grievous beyond bearing . . .

He peered into the darkness, he sought some sign. The master seemed turned to stone; man or Buddha? His stillness was that of a planted flower, alive in the winds, in the stillness, in all weathers.

"Traveling securely, protected by darkness . . ."
Death's underground, all its analogates.
He went into the deepest, the last of these, to which all others in life turn their gaze imploring; speak of us.

If we ask what it is like to be poor, to be despised, to be cast out, to be imprisoned, we are in fact asking, what is it like to die. In the old legends, to die is not to face extinction. Aeneas "descended into hell." He passed, menaced among gorgons, chimera and monsters. It was a herculean underground; the hero must wrestle, win release to upper air.

Of Jesus the rumors are gentler. It is said he encountered throngs of shadowy people, the heroes, martyrs, victims of all former times, waiting for him to open the gates of paradise. How long O Lord? We are to imagine a universal bread line perhaps, or the waiting room of a public dispensary, crowded with the ill and aged. But this image is on close scrutiny (more especially for those who must stand within it) too severe, too harried. The myth speaks of people in no great pain or discomfort, mainly waiting.

55

The word liberation is important. After his agony and death, Jesus "surfaces" once more to move among his friends, to join their brotherhood. We cannot be over-attentive to this, his considerateness and compassion.

He is at pains to assure them: I am he. This is not to be construed as a simple reassertion of identity, a joining of hands, the erasure of death, his saying, now friend will be with friend forever, death is swept aside.

No. Nothing soft-minded or pathetic or insinuatingly heroic. No gentle protagonism, no elbowing aside of the disciple, so he himself can stand full stage, at center.

What is here; he takes responsibility for his life and death. He asserts his conviction (literally undying) as to its rightness and continuity. More; he opens an interior door, at the back of the mind; an unsuspected entrance or exit (it is not clear; which one, both?). He invites them to walk through, "traveling securely, protected by darkness . . ." He is coiling a spring, the lax spring of history, of destiny.

If he deserves the name liberator, it is first of all to be applied to the imagination. He offers ways, apertures, lights them up, smashes them open even to let in air. He is fiercely anti-proprietary where the human stalemate, its stale air, are in command. We must see him in a kind of nightmare frenzy, moving like a madman down the dry arteries of time, tipping over the dessicated properties of the dead, invading the coffinmakers' shops, setting Caesar's coins spinning into corners to lie among the bat turds, ringing the tocsin, crying up the dead under pretext of fire, flood, shipwreck, Hamlet's father's murder, the disappearance of the town children into a mountain in company with a ragged flute player . . . Any excuse will do, any catastrophe; since any, or all together, are the sum meaning of any moment of time. Which is to say, men lie stiff in their shrouds and chin wrappings, and call it living, because now and then, at a creak in the earth's vaultings under a night wind, one or another of them is granted a wraith's dream; that it is autumn, and he walks hand in hand with a child, that he chooses among good and bad things like a living man, that he is married again to a woman, in the way of two bodies. Mild dreams of demihumans! No; most cruel and accurate, the living who are dead, the dead who are no different from what they were, the extension of the empery of the dead to the half-dead.

It is his wounds which count; not merely as points of identity, a birthmark or scar. He could care less; is he to move among men like a pensioner, a whining publican, begging the favor of their attention to his body paint, roses and wounds? No, these are points of heroic conduct, take them or leave; let the distracted powers pass him by, take their own soundings, left right left right, company halt, lie down in the dustbin among the bat turds.

Emblems of the new man. He is silent as his wounds. Only silence written there, they invite one "within." Untranslatable, he has tossed away the rosetta stone.

Men today are divisible into two tribes, according to ambition. (1) wants as soon as he has a few bucks ahead, to order the Ten Commandments tattooed on his bung hole, in ten colors. He will then back into eternity, doubled

over, virtuously visible, like a Near Eastern slave. (2)
wants the American flag tattooed in three colors, on his
prick's round. Thus even the most occult, far-reaching or
prosaic uses of that variable instrument can be quickly
validated. Pantagruel above Paris with inflated bladder,
Lord Chesterfield in his cutaway, a French sado-maso,
Reverend Father Minister Rabbi of the White House
Worship Staff, limp as a worm with worship; one is ready
to meet his maker!
from slavery to the tao
from amnesia   distraction   illusion
from dread   from despondency
from *horror mundi*   cuffs   autos-da-fé autobahns
from the cyclic wheel   from hell
from overlords   underdogs
from buried ears   boiled eyes
from talk   chalk   jabber and wocky
from *from*
deliver us

A Brief Pause a Refreshment in the Course of
Which the Master Will Address Us. All Are to
Be Seated According to Previous Suggestions in
That Position Most Like a Flower. These Conun-
dra Apothegms Strophes Epiphanies Are to Be Re-
ceived Gratefully Absorbedly as an Open Flower
a Night Rain. The Recurrent Image It Will Be
Noted Is That of Darkness. We Are Not to Fear.
All * Resisters Monks Flower Children Sun and
Star Gazers Brothers and Sisters * and Those Who
Within Themselves Betray Reprove Fail of Heart
Rant Bleed or What Is of More Serious Moment
Resign Themselves All Are Respectfully Urged to
Inhale Absorb the Dark as a Rose a Night Salt

Laden Fog It Is in Welcoming This Universal Element We Stand Within   Rest Within   and Rise Emboldened by the Truth

The second part of this night which is faith
Faith is comparable in quality of darkness to midnight;
deepest   darkest
. . . the perfect union that follows upon the passing of
the third night.
. . . more interior   more obscure   faith blinds the light
of reason
This superabundant light of faith is blackest darkness
overwhelms and eclipses the light of the understanding

. . . things which we have never seen nor understood   since
there is nothing which resembles them
Faith comes from hearing
unless you believe   you will not understand
faith is indeed a dark night to the soul   it imparts light
to the soul
man must be in darkness in order to have light on this road

. . . like a blind man   finding in dark faith   his only
support light   guide
make yourself blind in this manner   remain in total
darkness

do not walk by way of understanding   or inner feeling
or joyful sensation or imagination   but believe

pass beyond the highest things   to a state of unknowing

Make no more use of particular ways or methods
whether of perception understanding   feeling   so you will
bear within yourself

all possible ways   owning nothing   possessing all things

Gospel: I have come into this world as a crisis
that those who are blind should see   and those who see
should be struck blind

Now If You Will Please in This Darkness Choose
Your Image of the World Inhabit It Walk Within
It Peaceably or Run Like Hell the Other Way.

(1)   A plague-ridden ship succored by the presence and
voice of its captain, an anti-hero, it is said. Each
day the dead are decently buried at sea, infants are
born, the sick, for whom the choicest rations are
placed aside, are served, washed, fed, cared for with
utmost tenderness.

His nightlong meditations place him in commun-

The decks are foul, the sea is pure. It is an endless
savanna of sanity, it laves the ship with promise,
palpable as the tongue of an animal upon a fever.
The captain believes.

ion with a mysterious dolphin who swims the ship's wake. On occasion, he leaps behind the captain's eyes, leaving a track of St. Elmo's fire. He conveys greetings from other worlds, an inner sense of things, audacious promises; of which the sum is: fear not. He also offers the formula for a mysterious elixir, which spread on the tortured fevers of the ill, bring relief. (Unknown in origin to the ship's apothecary, the oil seems nothing more than a crude slick of liver of cod and haddock, unpleasant and of no curative value. Has something been added?)

The ship hastens for port, with the urgency of a wounded creature. While crisis endures and lives are at stake, the crew, passengers, the captain and his fiery shadowy alter are knit into a single being.

The longing of each of the living, multiplied by a mysterious X which dwells in the eyes of the captain, both crucifying and exalting, measures to the inch the distance between present agony and the port of call. That distance diminishes each day, the ship leaps on, the eye of an albatross, the energy of the horses of the sun.

We are one, they exult, even as they die, even as they commend the dead to the waves.

Mutiny, bloodshed, lust, envy, sloth, murder. Other voyages to come.

(2) The olive branch borne in the orange beak
of a dove, over a flood, from a promontory
where by inference, the deluge has
turned back, the olive grows
plentifully. Where?

(3)   The eyes of a child. The object of its inspection; a
lilac blossom. Not to be conceived as 1, 2, but as
both. Look into the child's inner eye. It is the
color of lilac. The blossom absorbs meantime in 5
seconds like five drops of rain 5 words to convey
the world.

   (4)   A matter breath-taking utopian supremely
impractical given the physiognomy of the
world. A swan. The problem: she hides her
ugly webbed feet; she hisses in distaste as you
read to her the Webster definition of her toes
(solution): *practical appendages for land and
water locomotion and for launching from
and reception back to land.* Thus through her
despised moles, pads and bunions, a creature
of three elements.

(5)   A prehistoric six-foot curled horn, its convolutions
those of a sea shell, the sea in motion, the arc of
space that dizzies the mind, lying like the breadth
of Blake's cosmic giant, between choice and choice.
It is the reveille of the tribe, its colors the striations
of a complex imperfect quartz, its inner coil, that
of ear, earth, or music itself.
                    It blares.   Choose!

   (6)   A golden orange stamped: Hesperides. Tegument, a living cooling suede; beneath, seeds,
a drenched pip. A vessel held in the hands of
a hero, filled at the amphora of dawn.

(7)   Andean fabrics, dyed in animal and flora colors.
Olà!

(8) Haute cuisine from Lapland.

(9) 500 Rent-A-Toilets for ice fishermen; to sit, shit,
     and take their quota quick.

(10) Cadillacs big as Pullman coaches for the funeral
     catafalques of Texas oilmen. Lower the whole rig.
     Pace.

     (11) APES build cages for Rhesus monkeys
           who are (apes say)
           both strange and familiar enough
           to merit the Sunday PM interest
           of urban apes and their spring-offs.
           The RMs hunt for lice
           in surgically clean cages
           and masturbate with ardor
           even in off season.
           They are thus (writes Professor AP)
           an indispensable link
           to recessive practice and malpractice
           long vanished from our people

(12) Attend to the cover of an earthen jar in a market in
     Jamshedpur, India. Musical sounds. The cover is
     rattled off from within. A hooded cobra ascends,
     weaving, sardonic, its gorgeous banded colors inflat-
     ing like a grin. Attention; music, serpent, brain of
     the serpent. It knows, better than the fingertips of
     the musician, the infinitely complex numerology
     of that music. One step more, one uncoiling, one
     skin shed, one insensate leap of that inflamed in-
     telligence. The universe will crash down, a colossus
     stricken by those fangs.

(13)   dentures   citations   medals   rosettes
            reveilles   fly shit   snot   matted bandages
            calves   liver
            rat tails
matters too small for summoning of general
conflagrations
        live with   put up with   parse and forget
        a public school 3rd grade textbook
Jane and John and their Cat   cutouts and their
    clothing

(14)   ENVY
        That sour-pussed broomstick virgin
        prurient about purity
        her hopeless chest full of unmentionable
        subject   verbs   objects
        dangling modifiers
        internal gerunds
        eyes; automatic ice trays
        tongue; stalactite
        Prescription for heavenly joy;
        (wintry) hopes for
        hottening up by hot-water bag or
        that failing
        and presupposing
        S. Sulpice plaster privates; Jesus

(15)   A madhouse at full moon. Return again and again
        after favorable prognosis, regrettable alas
            recurrence there   amid deviant cries   remove
            the trepanned cover   from the cranial
                                            jar
                dip the vessel deep in the cold moon
                                            well
                taste: bile   sourest lees   the death shriek
                of Christ's clotted lung
        yes and burgundy there; of the world's hung vine

66

*A Man Must Be Like a Blind Man Finding His
Only Support in Dark Faith   Taking It as His
Light and Guide   and Leaning upon None of the
Things Which He Understands   Enjoys   Feels
and Imagines*

The above are literally the words of our guru, a Western
man forsooth, therefore presumably in touch with all those
techniques, plug ins, systems, by which Western enlighten-
ment has not only lit up the West, but very nearly blown
up the East as well.

In the house where all cry out I see! and proceed to do
the works of darkness and death, there is one classic action
open to the wise; strike yourself blind, and explore that
kingdom.

It is the ying yang of wisdom; the truth of East and West

meet, in irony, in denial, in the great *no* offered the powers and dominations. It is one way of resistance open. Save your mind, save your reason.

There is in the neighborhood where I write this a teaching center for the blind. There, one may see in the springtime, blind people venturing forth with the first leaves, their sticks tapping the pavement, each in company of a guide, to help them cross streets, manage in public, liberate their other senses. It is both pathetic and evocative. The blind are exploring that nether kingdom of the spirit whose breadth will be that of their whole lives.

Their experience speaks to me, and my guides, who dwell by their dedication at the edge of sight, at the edge of blindness, resisting the kingdom of the blind, holding to the kingdom of faith—in decency, in the future, in what man may make of himself and his *communitas*.

What are the skills that must be learned?

To live with one's self. To survive. To exist in strongly human fashion, by actuating other senses and skills, often in the common life of man, grown dormant under the press of normalcy and routine.

Most of us live, we are told, with only some 30 or 40 per cent of our spiritual capacities in action. We apply little heart, little wind, little reflective power to the realities which press in upon us. What might man be today, what might his structures look like, if man were man? We hardly know, we hardly dare to know. We find our level, and drift with the current. In that current, foul or seductive or both, crowded with the debris of catastrophe, the pollution of ignorance and sloth (Pharaoh's dead horses and horsemen, the sticks and stones of battle, the roped bodies of prisoners), we lash together a life raft and climb aboard, saving what we can. It can hardly be called living; but at least it is not yet death.

At least, we comfort ourselves (cold comfort) it is not yet death. The sight of a blind man, the sight of a funeral cortege, awakens an ironic gratitude, bleak and self-blinding. I am not deaf or dumb, I am not a paraplegic, or a corpse. There is that to be grateful for. I am not a suppurating leper, I am not part of that vast bloodied clot of humanity which clings to the slums and dumping grounds of the third world, and the second, and the first.

Yet it is necessary to become in measure, in spirit, all these things, which are the common fate of man, the dark side of the human soul, the common soul, the unexplored, untouchable reach of grief and misery. To touch which is in all irony, to be reborn.

It is by contemplation one comes on this wisdom. A man is urged to bring his soul to stillness, to renounce the feverish amassing of gimmicks whose possession goes by the curious name "standard of life," to enter the dwelling of his spirit, whose figure is the dark hovel of the poor. To familiarize himself with that poverty, to live easefully and at peace there. To shut out the contrary din and enticement of pride, public notice, distraction. At that moment, the law of opposites, so dear to the wise, begins to exert its subtle pressure and force. To the many, oppose the few, and finally the one. To the violent superficial rhythms of life at the surface of life (violent in proportion as they are superficial) oppose the single tegument and movement of love.

The full irony is yet to come. To embrace this weird

69

absurd life of contradictions, is in fact to stand one's spirit on its feet, to get it moving on the road of change . . . So the Israelites in Egypt, so the blacks who draw on the same imagery. The movement is spiritual and therefore of the substance of universal history; it is necessary to say this. If you are a slave, become conscious of slavery by tasting it; no deliberation is required, most men are in that state, by birth or choice. Taste it for a while, deliberately, through others, brothers and guards and owners. Let your eyes roam over the whole landscape; see how human (?) life is arranged around that one project; the enslavement of men, narcoticizing or forbidding them to become conscious of the truth of their lives. Assess the price paid to retain the arrangement. Then, the price required if the arrangement is to end. The first is a matter of power; so, in a far different mode and method, is the second.

Life today is pushing these reflections very far. There is going to be little freedom until certain men have experienced prison. There is going to be little newness of life until good men have suffered—and a few of them have died. There will be few men (or none at all) capable of reading the Gospel, until men become skilled in reading the texts of events—and ordering their lives accordingly.

What I propose is by no means a self-indulgent question of solace for the afflicted, etc. It has to do with a purposeful entry into the realities of life, revealed in its oppositions and absurdities, within and without, in the spirit, in politics, in professions, in the churches.

The revolutionary quest, according to the hypothesis of guru John, is nothing more than the quest for moral change.

Such a vision, it need not be added, has little in common with the yapping and fawning of the B. Graham school. Nobility, rigor, absurdity, hunger and thirst, ecstasy, blood, apotheosis! The translations that work their way into consciousness of man today are more spectacular, in a sense even haphazard and outrageous, compared to in the way of a work of art, his words set up waves that continue to gather force, strike and ebb away once more.

Darkness Darkness Darkness How About
Some Light?

Just finished reading a long cursive monologue of Cleaver.
Just finished also a long (-er) study of Bonhoeffer. Also
Goodman, Apollinaire, Vallejo, Marcuse. A plethora of
riches. Some light, some contradiction, some dark.

1) The modesty required in order to include opposition
as an element of integration. Even such an opposite as a
tyrant who makes the revolution possible. The prison
makes the free man.

2) It was right and just for Cleaver to go slow on Martin
King. At times today the debased fashion is: bury him
again, deeper. This seems most scandalous of all when it
issues from so-called black revolutionaries, who have

fathered in their lives, maybe one idea and five basic words. Cleaver has more courtesy and sense; the sense at least to take it easy on a good man. He sees something that can't be easily touched, a long loneliness, something added to a balance that is not yet seen, a mystery. He is right.

3) What has Cleaver not yet seen? the long haul of history, of which the short haul is one element, one prize. Martin heard other voices, he was after a longer race and goal. No one should allow the "revolutionaries" to make a nigger of him, in contempt. The question they still have to deal with, before the people, is: what is a revolutionary anyway?

4) What do a few men draw on, to live and die less unwell than most men? Cleaver is haunted by this, in his better moments. He is wise to go slow.

5) Religion has a bad taste in his mouth, even while his attitudes are in the main, religious. It is by now a cliché to say, religion is part of the problem. It is another thing to say it cannot be part of the solution. That is a denial of historic fact; the fact of saints and heroes, who got man started, and died for it. Use your binoculars. Read some poetry. Read the documents. Don't despise the saints, including King.

6) The foregoing includes my brother, Phil, and the other jailbirds, of whom Cleaver has been one. More: jail was Cleaver's first field of force, his educator. He knows too little to exclude anyone from his call for coalition; least of all those who in their time and place, and drawing deep on their own traditions, find themselves at his side.

7) I find it particularly delicious to be reading Cleaver,

speaking to newsmen in Algiers, cooped up (as am I) in a domestic closet, facing the same onrush of sick power as he, hearing the same bad news and lies drumming in my ears. Cleaver is fond of saying the revolution is not a matter of one man's solution; it is a matter of the people 1) making the revolution, as the first and present task, and 2) being heard from in the new forms of life the revolution will forge. He'd better hear from us, better listen to us.

8) Beyond rhetoric about guns, pigs, confrontations, is the cooling off which contemplation makes possible, the necessities it actuates in human beings, that they come on new resources, in situations where only the man who stands at his full power and peak of love, can make any real difference. The precipitate of human outrage boils over, in a healing way, only when everything in man has been poured into the brew. Rage is indispensable to the new precipitate; so is compassion. Cleaver, but also Martin King.

9) The conflagration is rising. It is to the credit of men like Cleaver, Malcolm X, King, that they knew it, and said so. One is not thereby being apocalyptic or self-fulfilling or screwed up. One is merely reading the news and allowing the mind its proper function; which is not to sedate the powers of man, but to offer evidence for proper action, befitting reality. Martin King saw the fires kindling; he had another method than black power for fighting the fire; the point is, he fought it too, heroically, to death. Very few have measured the insight and courage required, in the heat of the civil rights struggle, to point to Vietnam. In effect King was risking all his people's gains in

order to include a distant people in his defense of life and freedom. Now it is a commonplace to say Vietnamese and American blacks are common victims of a common American method. But who first made the realization possible, whose leap was it, in the midst of the contrary advice of lesser men—including black at that?

10) Self-defense: a keystone of Panther struggle. "Take up, use arms skillfully!" At a former stage of things, King went unarmed; in a sense he invited personal disasters. The Panthers accuse him of even more folly than that. A kind of ideological retardation of black people, keeping the truth about their lives from them, about the monstrous character of the forces they must deal with. Cleaver calls it something like the "plantation mind." Unjust, an over-simplification if there ever was one. The point is that King led them out, the first exodus of the impoverished disenfranchised people in their entire American history, masses of people taking hope once more. He awakened the best in them, moving toward the highest expectations of those who were barring the way. Who is to say that such hope, embodied and rendered heroic by one man, does not actually create a new face in the enemy? We are in deep waters here.

11) But, they say, he's dead. And so is non-violence. Another scene is here; guns. *Primum est vivere;* the first task of the sane man is survival. (Are they conscious that such a slogan is saleable, like arms, to anyone with the dollars to buy, on the world market? Israel, Egypt, South Africa, Mozambique, Brazil, etc., etc.) Indeed the force of the slogan reaches far and wide and down and down, into

revolutionaries and racists, into the rat holes of the world; rodents sharpen their teeth on it as well as heroes.

12) The non-violent hero often ends up dead. So, avers Cleaver, does the revolutionary. So does the American soldier, by the thousand. Death being cheap and common to the point of bathos. An interesting question, however, remains: who dies in a way which is a gift to history? who makes it less inevitable that many others will die, in the same way, in even larger numbers, in the next generation?

13) To take up weapons is to lose one's choice of weapons. Men who take up the sword, die by the sword. Militants object to such language on many counts; on some of which they are correct. But they must also understand something of the literary form here; the sayings are a kind of shorthand, a prophetic shock tactic. (In somewhat the way hot ghetto language is.) They warn, and the warning has a long evidence, of the itch, always present in an irritated body, to treat symptoms as causes, to use the gun as universal solvent. When that principle is embraced, the revolutionary meets the oppressor; a common image in the mirror, each aping the other.

14) There is this danger about self-defense. In proportion as it becomes a full-time occupation, it tends to seize on the attention, the vocabulary, to seize upon speech in a way that affects all behavior, makes everything else subordinate. This leads to only one message; a full-time obsession with death. In time, the language becomes the reality; one believes what he hears and says and repeats. "National security" comes to require, and to justify, genocide.

Witness, for instance, the progressive seizure of American international policy by U.S. generals. Toward the end of his term, Johnson, we are told, never met his advisers on any serious policy question, without the presence of one or more of the chiefs of staff. Nixon is protesting congressional limitation of funds for the war, pleading that such action endangers his prerogatives as commander in chief of the armies. His pinstripe suit is in fact a thin disguise; he represents quite openly the militarization of the government function, domestic and abroad. This is called simply self-defense; domestically, "law and order"; abroad, protection of our troops, etc.

15) There is a cruel lesson here for revolutionaries, too. Concentration on the sights of a gun inevitably contracts the bore of the mind. How does one keep the mind open to the full range of action possible to its powers? That range of action includes, in the nature of things, respect for the central position of non-violence, even (most of all) in a time totally and officially dedicated to violence. Lives must be defended and protected, yes; but what do we do with *our* lives? To this question, the gun cannot speak. Can the gunman?

16) There is some evidence that he can, provided he is first of all a peaceable man, a man of his people. Guevara, Ho, Castro. Each at different stages, in different ways, won historical attention to their analyses and actions. With good reason. I would venture to say each is deserving of praise, of being serious agents of life and liberation, in proportion as he assiduously placed limits on violence, and made the creation of human structures his main life task. Conversely,

the task is tarnished in proportion as one invokes violence as exemplary, as inevitable, as central, etc.; or failed to mourn for bloodshed (on either side), or failed to issue stern rules concerning humane treatment of prisoners, etc.; or permitted torture, or filled prisons, etc. Revolutionaries are heroic and praiseworthy, in proportion as they surpass the methods of the enemy, and teach the people to do the same—even at times of great tension and danger, when the provocation to forfeit lives, to take revenge, is greatest. Note in this regard the North Vietnamese release of American prisoners, together with their insistence that no reciprocal gesture was to be admitted. (The political gain consequent on such actions is of course enormous; and justly so.)

17) Acculturation to violence as the ordinary way to conduct one's business. In proportion as this occurs, other options open to men, other ways of settling their differences become extra curricular; the main diet being human meat.

Wherein a Series of Contradictions Is Pointed Out in View Perhaps of a Resolution of Truth

According to practically every Zen master who ever wrote
    anything
it would have been better to write nothing.
They expend a gread deal of ink praising the *tabula rasa*
upon which the divine may trace his austere lines
the mind which is pure lotus before weather,
    pure unknowing before knowledge
        and which, rather than migrate, wander, rap, socialize
    or raise hell against the hell raising around them

        keeps wiping itself clean of time and its slick,
            muck, smog, mist.

the world, the theory goes, attaches itself to the mind
        only in such form—beclouding, smirching

79

that pure crystal of admirable behavior; the soul

which otherwise, otherwhere, otherwhen
          a better more supple instrument

          of love, knowledge and intuition,
     would in the manner of a gorgeous box kite, ascend,
          dip, taste the sun, startle beholders with its
     exquisite audacity
                    mimic in fact
the very rhythms of the spiritual universe
                              making of man
          as was once said
                    "the measure of all things."
I must confess to you certain deep-seated reservations with
     the classic theory, as stated.

          In the first place
     it seems fairly clear that Zen texts should consist
of blank sheets of handmade paper
               page after page fanning out in the hand
to release like the cards of a prestigitator
          those numinous presences
               alike and most unlike
     birds   poets   flowers   desires   light inhibitions
whose exorcism is the gentle and liberating task
               of the masters of the soul.

     Such not being in fact the case.

     The case being in fact; that we dwell in the world
          where even the most aerial spiritual counsels must
               strike up and against
               real and unabridged men.
     The case; monks too dwell in bodies   bodies occupy
          space
               require light   air in the scrofulous world
where these goods and services formerly

flowed like a Niagara
were ample as a mid-Pacific
Now no longer; the contrary pressures being cruel
to all who claim
the honor of being man
and wear far more significant
than saffron or brown sack
the stigmata, hands feet and side
inflicted by the round of—say—4 seasons, one spouse
3 children, 1 Biafra, and the nightlong daylong yearlong
nightmare to be viewed through the crenellated
interstices (filed to a shark's point) of the
mouth of a Chief of Staff or (the choices are
not large)
through the lumpy smile creaking with
ineptitudes and inhumanities
of a Secretary of Defense. I say Vietnam.

Therefore and therefore;
it follows naturally if somewhat illogically
(illogic being the heart of logic when robes
wear monks and Zen masters write texts on the
ineffable)

the process is not through a simplicity to
simplicity
as though one were born without eyeballs
ears nose and throat
not to say crotch
strictly standard equipment
for navigating Pike's Peak, the Mojave Desert
and all the ships at sea
No, we must take it "all in all, a man"
as I think I recall Hamlet says
in another context
or perhaps the same.

If simplicity is attained (it cannot be presumed) it will only

81

be because we have won high points in the endurance
race;
  HAVING DANCED ON OUR feet for four hundred
    hours, barefoot, on live coals and come forward
      chest out and smile on to face the cameras   bear-
      baited and unbeat

  HAVING BEEN AWARDED a bum's citation by
      Commander in Chief of Song My
        for holding one's nose while the flag dipped
        and the band blared
                  and the children twitched and
                  bled like a mound of calves' liver
                  newly excised from the innards
                  flung in a ditch there among the
                  armed heroes at attention
                    in a Rose Garden ceremony

HAVING BEEN TESTED in our mortal frame by the
application
        direct or by absentee ballot
        of certain new and hitherto undreamed of
        blessings of technologized imagining
            to wit

      mace   cuffs   restraining belts   holes   marshalls
    marsupial courts   rhesus judges   fines   denials of bail
            HAVING EMBRACED the supposition of
the virtuous clown;
              . . . *anyone's flesh, his   hers   or theirs is*
              also mine
        OR
  . . . *who touches you with a cattle prod, sets me*
                uncontrollably screaming
      the pied imagination (whose nearest and dearest ana-
logue is the absurd wound of the slashed mouth)
              having for principle and prologue;
  The Seamless Nature Of That Cunning Web

(only to be seen in certain fleeting lights
    by a few, by changelings
by those skilled in a moment's grace; after rain, at
    dawn, at crepuscule)

HAVING COURTED such inanities
    as are sown like a dust storm scalding the seeing
                                                eye
            a germ warfare against burly health
        a sermon on the mount bleated by a loser
having endured in consequence
        the slings and arrows of construction workers
            building like good ants the Babylon of man
                (for lunch hour; a man hunt)
        HAVING BEEN, having very nearly been buried
        (man)

        HAVING KNOWN in plumage and pelt the
        slowing heart
                of the last handful of pink-billed herons
                in perpetual open season   moulting into
                death
HAVING RIDDEN UNEASY rider   or Jesus
bearing his cross
            the last mile

            After all this
        stuttering *etcetera* of horror
            the common life today
    of former   food gatherers   basket weavers   cave
                                                dwellers
a text which you
                dipping your chosen quill
                    in your own chills and fevers
    may amortize   blot   befoul   immortally descry
                                            illustrate

        The suggestion being

83

it is only the sipping and ingesting of such a
   witch's broth
bringing into play
   the fine gustatory discrimination of professional tasters
      of paté de fois
      his palate sharpened like a bat's radar a bee's
         sting
      on the world's flesh pots
         that gives historic density to the dictum; e.g.,
         "there is some shit I won't eat"

   Simplicity! The lotus gesture!
   There is a work by Jean Arp, called *Infinite*
      Amphora.
   The materials are so simple as to seem almost farcical;
      a wooden cutout of a limp disc
      gray; stuck on a light blue board.
   there are bulges like necks at opposite ends of the jug
      areas of white paint issue from these and stream
         off
         broadening as they go toward the edge and
         beyond.
      streams of what? we must say simply
         everything anything nothing
      light darkness seed spirit water
      It is a Zen image The jug of the universe
         The stream of creation The life of the mind.

      simplicity is composed (eventually)
of the dissidence and fury of the human frame
      that the lotus gesture
      inwardly composes accepts
         even as it resolutely sets limits

      to what?
      to that journey; its mischance its stages
                                    defeats

84

the graves that mark its portages
the skeletons mounded beside camp fires
the forgiveness also   the epiphanies
   the supervenient hope that fuels the heart
piercing the mirages   presenting in obscure
penumbra

the shape of things to come
which
it
makes
come

God Leads a Man Step by Step to the Greatest
Degree of Inwardness; or, Simplicity Is a Different
Matter From a Hatful of Watch Parts Which,
Grace of a Bavarian Grandpa, Has Become a
Watch

In a sense, yes, cut loose; in another, left dangling.

I look out on the leaves of a single tree in a backyard. It has accompanied my long-distance dash of the last weeks; all the frenzy and hilarity since Cornell.

It was standing dead as a pike staff, frozen in one of the gorges when I left that scene. I knew it there; it was part of the sublime untouched earth art, the enchantment of that place.

It raced ahead of me to Jersey like a witch's perambulating broom; fast, slick as a vapor trail, single-minded, even obsessive, like a witch's arrow. It wore no disguise; anonymous as a broom, peeled down to use, and wearing a wig.

I came and went, so did it. It migrated, it metamorphosed. It could stay around awhile, it could move on; it had gold and frontiers in mind even when there were no more handouts. Or consider; it had a commune just over the mountain: Paul Nat Jim Tom Jeff ud be around there too, there were high school kids and laid-off workers. You could always mix and rap with people lining up to get their welfare checks.

Support? What the hell does a tree need? You shake down where you can, there's always a friend.

You get busted across some cop's knee, they hate your hair they hate your talk they hate your guitar they hate your hate—of the war or the government or the powers. Watch out for the big plains the heartland the diners the sheriffs they're computerized by now; they take fingerprints, throw you in overnight, to wait for the hot word to come ticking back. If you're wanted anywhere in the world they'll know it on one half (½) hour sharp. If you sit there shivering and hear axes or carving knives being ground on sharpeners outside, that means the computers said: git him. It's known as new-style preventive-detention first-strike lynch mob. You'll love every minute of it esp. the view from the ridge which in this (most) town(s) is outstanding, a tourist attraction in point of fact.

Now if things come to this sort of pass; don't, repeat,

do not lose your cool. Second, do not insist on showing your B.A. degree, torn draft card, or the photo of the five of you messing around the Boeing plant, leafleting against war contracts. Not a bit; this is known officially as counterproductive; it reddens up the computers and brings on galloping apoplexy in sheriffs.

No. Play it cool.

Now supposing also that a tree has been the immemorial instrument of lynch mobs, even before computers baptized the instance, naming it socialized medicine, what have we to do?

It is to suppose; in the universe of ecological sanity, at which stand trees (at the very heart of) it is quite clear that any tree worth its salt, at the approach of another ecologically aware specimen mortally in danger, will recoil. Or some equivalent, translated.

The nearest likeness we can come on, from our vantage point (which is that of cockroach extermination applied like mace to the four winds and seasons) is those workshops they often hold in the movement, consisting of some fifty brave souls who are about to do a study with foundation backing (their own foundations, their lower spinal backing) for the sake of oral (or anal) history, on how leather lead boots curses gases threats arrests affect or afflict the human spirit and arse and head and upper and lower arms and indeed kidney section. Such being an extremely valuable study not only for the movement, but for law-enforcing agencies; they too studiously perusing the statistics of such encounters with a view to improvement of equipment. Theirs being the glory of standing before history from the halls of Montezuma to this moment; AD SUPERANDUM BELLICOSOS SERVOS, bringing down the bastards who tried a slave revolt under Diocletian or Nero and never since quite got it out of their systems.

Well. One of the features of those workshops is a consistent stubborn effort to teach even the most crustacean vertebrate to go limp.

Simple. Somebody usually thinks to bring along two specimens to illustrate this. 1) A worm which already biologically speaking has passed the test and even wears a decoration from the movement; not only having been kept for bait in innumerable bleak tin cans but actually cut in half actually martyred for the movement and actually surviving by marvelous transmutations. That one is gentle as Mahatma at the loom, nakeder than he, and presumably in process of writing his memoirs. But comes out again and again, at need. 2) A land crab. Illustrative of the other side of things. He may seem, at first glance, singularly unfitted for this lesson. But just wait.

Well, we were approaching the Ridge where, according to all available computers, this agitating hunkering commie outsider is to be wiped out. Or strung up, more properly.

The posse crosses the superhighway (this ought to be an example to them creeps who race through here with out-of-state license plates letting off troublemaking out-staters) to the Ridge. Where Ol' Skull Tree stands, or they think it does, to dangle this blue-eyed darlin' high as his daddy years gone, swing him up like a watch fob on a gambler's thumb.

You don't say so.

What happens is, this tree's been at a non-violent workshop. Only the posse don't know. Spiritually speaking, on account of long hatefulness going back to their daddies and granddaddies and the kind of preaching at camp meetings that's seeped into guts like tobacco juice, they've all got broomsticks up their asses. Consequence, they would much rather break than bend, push come to shove.

Our hero approaches his hour; according to his momma's instructions, his lip is upper, and stiff. She always said, trees you can trust. Humans I don't know.

Her son believed, and was saved.

Keeping the matter short; they threw up the rope, it doubled down over the limb. The tree kept playing it straight. That is to say, give thieves an inch; the mile belongs to you.

All of a sudden our hero is there, heroic as John Wayne before the bug eyes of history's cameras. He don't give a damn, as the script says, he's ready for his maker.

Sudden, the tree goes limp as a shoelace, a worm. That limb, on which our hero was to drink the wind, bends at the shoulder. The whole act's off. Our hero runs free. So we have reason to believe.

In Which the Moral of the Preceding Is Discussed.

When I was in Hanoi, some two years ago, our friends took us to the National Museum, housed in a former French school for French children, the French, like all incursionists, having dispersed under the rain of fire eventually produced by that old concocter of bad weather for the unjust, known as The Equalizer, or simply, history.

There, I remember Buddha.

He was in many guises, from rags to riches and back again; from smiles to tears, from Jehovah to Job. It gave the goose pimples. He wore terrific smiles, induced by good food or the right prayers. Or he was the original Bone and Rag man, squatting with diurnal patience at the barred gates of the rich; you could almost hear by inference, the revelry just beyond his starvation, the neglect, the pain of hanging around the scene, the patience of the god, in face of leathery eyes and inhuman moneybags.

He was a slave impaled on the staffs of the Occupying Power; he lurked there in shadows, I swear he was under an air raid, his thin sticks drawn up to his thin belly, totally intent on the first business at hand; survival, an armadillo.

Or he sat there like a carved lotus, his hands modeled on that flower, his ecstatic closed eyes summoning the night of the senses. Like a jar, like a universe; he said, only come inside, sit down at peace with time and this world. More; all creation will stream from you, who have let it all go.

He was a veritable fountainhead. You had but to reach out, to turn him on. And to be turned on. To contain wisdom, to endure folly. To last it all out; from the Chinese through the Japanese through the French through the Americans it was all less than the wink of an eye less than the alighting upon one's eyelid of one of the multiple feet of a tropical insect which now came and now went and was in sum worthy of less attention than the pulse at the wrist or the beat of the indwelling heart.

My country 'tis of thee.

In our ears was the blaze of air-raid sirens, in our being the shame of the war. We had had certain lessons during that week; crouching in air-raid shelters, hearing the drone of lethal motors and the obscene thud of bucket upon bucket of wrath dropped by those pirate birds. Yes.

The many faces of the Buddha were the many faces of man; under perpetual fire, nearly extinguished, stubborn as the soil, drawing his skills and methods from the rhythms of wind and rain and sun. The people were the very embodiment of the land, its genius, its numen, spring from its furrows, armed (of necessity) to the teeth; the warriors of that landscape, the meditative perpetual poor men, perpetually at the mercy of, perpetually made an example of, perpetually violated, the subject of derision and folly and punitive action, a brushfire stamped out according to military dispatches. Or; gone underground, a smoke, a hint, a menace.

Buddha; all this while the United States of America was taking an Infant Jesus to its religious heart, changing His underpants on major feast days. A culture of infancy savored and prolonged; a religion for infants.

The changeful face of the Buddha, his thousand arms touching the extremities of the spiritual universe; embracing all, including all.

I thought; we have missed the mark. The Long Sleep, nirvana, belongs to infancy, to us. The face of Buddha is the face of man, tortured, stricken, inward, ecstatic. The simplicity is that of man dwelling in his manhood, man who has swallowed fire, and lives.

We had caught a glimpse; men have seen less than we, and arisen, determined to be men.

It was a question of perspective; of seeing, on the large loom of history, something of pattern and form. Some way out of a corner, into which bad policy, refusals of life, Western fanaticism, religious frenzies and murderous anti-humanism, had shunted us—almost all of us.

It was necessary to give ourselves away; to place our-selves where we belonged, in mankind. To place our lives in a larger continuum of action and inwardness. To allow the Buddha to shape our features.

One is not at all sure how this is to be done. But one is at least sure of how it is not to be done. A man is forbidden to make capital of the death of other men. To make war as men make war today is so obscene a violation as to destroy us in the very decision, in the very first stages of the debate.

We are required to stand firm upon a few such principles, as though the ground beneath our feet were indeed a rock, as though we were fired and set there, in bronze. Thus, in order to stand with man, it is necessary to speak our *no* to the anti-men, the moral midgets, the mad powers.

To save the earth and those who dwell upon the earth and those who love and tend the earth, and those who inherit the earth and bequeath the earth to children, and those who contemplate the earth and draw upon its ener-gies and beauty and surprise; in order to make poetry, in order to make love, in order to make sense. It may be nec-essary to go under the earth. To go underground. To join that vast network of the unborn and the dead. To resign from America, in order to join the heart of man.

I speak, of course, of plain fact; of my own case. But it seems to me that every real question opens every other question; every act, if it be genuine (which is to say, both integral with one's own life and with an eye to one's brothers), opens a whole arterial system of analogies.

I mean to say something quite simple and practical. It

94

is useful, indeed inevitable, that our lives endure a certain perplexity. It is neither useful nor inevitable that our lives be stuck fast in moral stalemate.

Stalemate. Some Americans, in this time and place, in this year of this war, can do nothing more than repeat the stale gestures of two, three years ago. Appeals to the President on the occasion of the latest international outrage, letters (dead letters) to powers and dominations (dead powers), etc., etc. The problems are thereby objectified; they are never personally assumed. Methods and tactics continue to rest on dead assumptions like a stale sandwich in the teeth of a corpse; e.g., that the powers are moral in intent, and respond to moral appeal, that governance lends its ear to thoughtful citizens, that the military, in its resources and policies, is the instrument of sane men in the family of nations; no more apt to be used as instruments of violence (in fact no more useful) than, say, the helmet of an unarmed London bobby.

Now when such assumptions continue to be hauled in to save one's sanity (or better, one's security) the ethical life becomes flaccid and palsied before realities, themselves charged with demonic energy and inventiveness. Indeed the demons flourish on the dead meat of the well-intentioned.

I am no more sure than others of what may be the physiognomy of the "new man." But I am sure his features are not those of the liberal whose politics are concocted out of despair, fear, dread of change, dread of loss. There is more to be done than work ourselves into tantrums against a wailing wall.

What is to be done, in accord with the truth of things,

has something to do with the unmentionable fact of death.

And its analogies. Which are so to speak the political facts of life today; imprisonment, jeopardy, legal pressures, refusal of tax payments, refusal of war-related emoluments and jobs, etc., economic insecurity for one's self and family, refusal of induction (and concomitant; aiding and abetting), these and other long-term projects whose nature and scope the times themselves open before us. E.g., restructuring of family life, to render it less vulnerable to the warmaking state, more functional for resistance; new schools, to take children out of military and economic rat racing early; housing battles, rent refusals; getting one's immediate life in touch with the variety of peoples who, from diverse social backgrounds and needs, want change so badly they hurt. To render the movement less spasmodic and reactive; more on the move, more innovative. Realizing that whatever the nature of the next crisis (inevitably military, inevitably outrageous), one's understanding must take into account the long patient struggle ahead; take into account as well, the infinite capacity of American power to temper the wind (their firestorms) to the shorn lamb (the wretched of the earth). The principle goes something like this: those who make peace with whatever public outrage; the expansion of war, the death of Panthers, are thereby ready for whatever is to come—i.e., more death, more militarism, more racist extermination of helpless people. Or so to say: Things have been bad, but wait till you see tomorrow. Therefore, cheer up. And yet . . . and yet . . . In saying this, one has not said everything. Indeed something else must be admitted.

For, to say the least, some Americans have bowed out (or been kicked out) of the death game. Perhaps out of the worst, may arise the best. Perhaps? perhaps even to the point where the expression of a hope seems justified: out of America, even out of our crimes, may come the new man.

What will he be like? A man of integrity; which is to say, a man with two sides, inner and outer. A contemplative, intellectual, artist; a man of skills and worthwhile intention; a public man, whose life is on the line; whose moral sense includes the mysterious sense of when and how to die. When best, how best; with all the implications of that, for public weal, for the victims.

One thing seems sure; the new man will not spring from Jove's forehead. The gods, the true gods of man's history, of his worship, do not work miracles of debased magic, on behalf of the morally indolent. No; such a man will get born because he has trodden the furnace, and died there.

We may feel impelled to take a break at this point for cold comfort.

I mean this; practically everyone I know (let us limit the case to the movement) dreads the truths I have just stated. Dreads their being true, dreads their coming true, for him.

We walk, all of us, in this dread; in its nearly overmastering control of our lives and actions, its debased power over our motivation, its circuitous skill in putting a good face upon cowardice. Finally, its skill in turning men aside from the straight path of the truth, herding them into the squirrel cage of excuse, self-duplicity and damnation.

97

Clinging to the Husk of Sense (an Attitude Which Resembles the State of Childhood) a Man Never Attains to the Substance of the Spirit (Which Resembles the State of Perfect Manhood)

It is undoubtedly helpful to be modest about one's life; an attitude officially despised by many people, including generals, East side New York dog emporia, cops and the looks they cast upon hair and its proliferators, the dreams of most people in power (a goodie on the forefinger of God, a voice from the cloud enticing; come, more). Likewise the covert killers, who make harmless things on the side, and anti-personnel weapons in the main. And all those creators of Unconscious Irony, who commonly turn the front page of the NY *Times* into a riotous bloody collaborationist effort between Genet, Jesus, Pilate, a southern salt-pork sheriff named Imponderable Jim Clan, Aristophanes, and the head of John the Baptist, after excising of same; refusing to stay dead.

No, we are not a modest people. A straighter, more modest assessment of us could, I submit modestly, hardly be offered.

Occasionally, however, a modest question does get asked. And even more occasionally, answered. I remember being once cut up rather severely at a public gathering for attempting to answer one such question; do you then consider R. McNamara a war criminal? I said simply, yes. My interlocutor has not spoken to me since. Now I take it, my answer was modest, in the (neglected) sense that it attempted to place responsibility for actions alongside the authority which rendered a man in authority purportedly, answerable to Us, the People. Immodesty, in the instance, consisting in such vaporizing of the Yes and No of power as loses the issue beyond retrieving, somewhere in a chain of command. That attractive phrase! is it perhaps drawn from a gang of navvies unloading the ship of state of its noisome or luxurious cargo items—something for everyone, but mainly pacifiers, and Bread and Circuses?

I want in justice to pay tribute to the import of such questions. They are modest too, in the sense that they are right and just, whatever the spirit in which they are asked. We could do with more of them, in public debate, to the good of all citizens, who retain some residual sense of the mind of founding fathers, one of whose passionate

99

intentions evidently was to reduce to the vanishing point the divine right of rulers to be answerable only to God for their tyrannies against men. (Which is to say, inevitably, answerable to no one, the religion of most First Estate Members being what it has been, and is.)

No, they were insisting, there is a human scale of things, the violation of which in any form, leads to the violation of man's spirit itself. We might think for a moment, of architectural examples; the tomb of General Franco, the state government mall of the city of Albany, the public works and pomps of Mayor Frank Hague; and then of the speed with which true public modesty is scattered to the winds—the bulldozing of Resurrection city in D.C., when the poor attempted, in their huts and mud, to put their lives on display, for public shame and redress.

Often such modesty is a simple function of a sanity constantly seeking, in spite of great odds, to reassert itself against the imbalances and rampagings of power. The questioning of the war, and the style out of which the question arises is of point here. Legislators and businessmen ask the question, in one way. Is the war not immoral, unconstitutional, etc.? But their stance is wrong, and so the question is easily isolated and dealt with. There is a notable lack of indignation and passion in their reproaches. They are asking merely that a mote be removed from the virtuous eye of the nation, that the inflammation of public weal be reduced, and the seeing eye go on seeing things—as they are. The protest is immodest, proceeding as it does from self-interest and a stake in an unjust system, which stake is plunged deep as an oil well or a land claim in foreign soils—the rights of the native being, as usual, ignored in principle.

"Clinging to the husk of sense . . . resembling the state of childhood." Such language is not merely a primitive reading of child psychology; rather, I take it, the statement attempts an acute reading of the fact of childishness, of regression. Americans supposedly, at one revolutionary stroke, freed their souls from all magical attachment to objects, forms and symbols of power as would indicate coercion and control over human beings. The intentions were admirable, and in their virile first-generation effort, probably genuine; they did offer human beings a new start and lit a beacon of hope on our shores. Alas, not for long.

What shortly arose, as Whitman, Thoreau, Emerson, Melville and others were to announce in the nineteenth century, was a new form of oppression fathered by American secularized power. Kings and popes were no longer of interest; they had been pushed from the center stage. Now the interests of a new class were urgently pressed, in the course of industrial awakening and the opening of world markets to free enterprise. Who was to rule the new world? It was manifestly not to be "the people" in any recognizable sense, a sense briefly created by the fervor of revolution, here, in France, and eventually in Russia and China. No, if that had been the case, a welcoming hand would surely have been extended from frontier to frontier: from the homesteaders and emancipated slaves and indentured servants and labor movements and ethnic interests here, stretching as far as was required into the awakening world of man.

Something else occurred. In a sense, little short of tragic, none of these revolutions was a clean break: every one bore along with it the tide of self-interest and privilege from which it seemed to free itself. The Puritans exterminated Indians, the Maryland gentlemen bought and sold Africans, the shopkeepers and tinkers patented and protected their cotton gins and combustible engines. Someone was always left in the cold; someone, in principle, didn't make it. That someone, invariably, was black, brown, red, yellow, newly arrived on the scene, poor, uncouth; his accented speech gave him away; he challenged the economic pork barrel as a private domain; he wanted to organize his own ilk; he was violent, ill-advised, presumptuous. Maybe, also, he didn't believe the common assumptions about progress, success, the heady doctrine of hegemony, urban growth, the sanctity of private property, personal initiative, the virtuous exportation of American vision. Maybe he didn't believe the marines should land here or there or anywhere. Maybe he didn't believe in annexing lands and people like natural if unwilling accretions of empire. Maybe he didn't believe that Mexicans, Indians, blacks, Alaskans, belonged in something called The Union—before they had been heard from, before an elective choice. Maybe he wasn't in trouble?

Such beliefs, engendered by inhuman treatment on these shores, were sometimes dealt with bloodily and abruptly. (We are just beginning to understand something of this, in our neglected reading of black history—what might be called the unpublished history of the American poor. Such reading gives one to pause, as the French would say.) We put down slave revolts and contained the labor movement in the course of several of the bloodiest skirmishes in modern history. What we did to the Indians has been so thoroughly sprayed with Mystic Glo paint, the realities of the struggle have been so mythologized and distorted, that it is very nearly impossible to get to the truth of things. Then too, there are few Indians left to tell their side of it.

National immodesty thus is fed by national amnesia. This was indeed my portion, my schooling; I was advised to look down my nose at all those rioting French and Italians and even Germans (the Scandinavians and British seemed the only sanely constituted people, their cool heads firmly in place on non-violent limbs). And then there was of course ourselves. How virtuous, how temperate, how altruistic, how peaceable we had always, invariably, been. How modest, in sum, before the prevaricating, squabbling, land-grabbing, empire-building, war-racked "others"! How was I to see the blood on us? It was thoroughly expunged. How clean mother's hands were! it was the cry of Lady Macbeth's offspring, the cry of the sons of Mother America.

The "husks of sense" may not be the "substance of spirit"—but for a long time they made up the only diet most of us knew. That was before blacks came along with their historical "soul food" diet—composed of guts and hoofs and ears and jowls of animals, the food cooked in slavery, far from the sirloin beefeaters in the big house on the hill. The blacks served up the truth; a mess of it. The odors drift uphill, even into the big house, to its sons and daughters. The truth, the brutal force of a lightning bolt. How come no one told us all this? you mean the system has been that wrong, that bloody, that murderous, that greedy and callow? for that long?

From out of sight, to insight. From out of mind, to what?—sanity? One thing is fairly certain; the big house on the hill is going to have a hard time hanging on to its clapboards, paint, roof and walls. The truth is out; the sons are in rebellion. They're meeting by night in some ditch or outhouse, conniving with niggers, against the outriders and owners. Against their fathers. Slave rebellion? It's more, and less. When the sons of the slaves are planning with the sons of the owners to take over the plantation, Americans need a new word, for a new reality . . .

"The substance of the spirit, which resembles the state of perfect manhood." I like the phrase, probably because I understand it so imperfectly. It seems though to gather in by implication many of the almost insupportable ironies that burden our air today. Free, abounding, modest, embodied, plain of speech, witty, various in style from hair to love play, making a culture almost in spite of itself, a culture by happenstance; politically edgy, often enraged, often simply wrong in statement and assessment, on occasion thoughtless, cruel, at enmity with the good; the sum favors the left of the ledger.

I think the phrase of John also bears on the irrepressible utopianism that figures so large in the American grain. We had quite forgotten our horror-ridden history; in a

Freudian sense, we had sublimated it; in a religious sense, we had absolved ourselves. Then the skeleton, beyond human explaining, walked again—in the house. He spoke, and he made sense—a sense long forgotten, falsified and mistaught. Now the truth comes rushing forward, with the power of a tidal wave, across peaceable lowlands. How will we cope with it all, and still save the house, save the possessions?

We will not. The young are acting out that loss, by deliberate good sense, by a free act; by giving it all up. They have made a choice, a renouncement, ahead of the cataclysm. So in a true sense, the apocalypse is robbed of its nightmarish fury; it has lost its power. The rehearsal for death has been so rigorous, so conscious, that death itself is transformed.

This is a good way to face the future; with empty hands. One almost says; this is the only way to cleanse the blood away; open your hands, it is the possessions which are bloody, it is the attachments, it is the keys and freeholds and liens and stocks. This is the umbilical web of "the state of childhood" which, uncut, stiffens into halter and rope.

I write this in a bad time, which for me is also a good time. Perhaps if I were more acute, more sensitive to my situation, I would cringe with dread. A man without a country, trapped within that country, with prison ahead.

What sort of bedeviled future is that, what sort of present? Your brother in jail, your life and its relationships ruptured, all that space the mind needs to be itself, to know its freedoms, to land its fish—gone. A shadow over life, the less than human life of the hunted.

I can only report, with whatever simplicity, looking into my heart—none of it matters. What matters is—to sow the future, and so to attain one's manhood. To keep on the trail and spoor of that utopia which is man's true and real estate.

The Understanding Should Not Feed upon Visions. Being a Meditation on a Special Edition of Life Magazine: to the Moon and Back.

The guru's opinion, quoted in the first part of the above headline, has to do with the destructive effect of trips taken in despite of man, man's just concerns, man's brothers. Moon trips, in fact and folly and metaphor. I came by chance on a special edition of *Life*, a heavy-coated extravagantly colored showcase for the space trip. Page after page of concentration on what is known popularly as "human interest." (What were the families of the heroes doing as their spouses swung aloft? What were they like, as boys, as adolescents, as men?) Highly charged, focused, dramatized; the body's Sahara, its abstract beauty, is plastered with the mod paint of pic and poetry. The just, austere sense of here and now, the tragic lives and deaths of the majority of men, all pushed to the edge of attention or compassion. The wastefulness of obsession and pride, the litter on the distant planet, the obscene symbols left there; the flag, ribbed with wire, to wave and wave like an articulated skeleton; on the memorial plaque, the lying words of peace, while back home men make war, as usual.

Back on earth, too, in the TV-dominated living rooms, the women and children watch their men make hay of history. Mod women, mod children and friends. There are no intruding blacks, no slogans, no variety, no other tensions than the one wound tight by the task itself, and the vulnerable arc that joins "national effort" to the nationals—white, right, dolls in the showcase window. The women wear mid-sixties hairdos and dresses, inspired by the couture of Jacqueline Kennedy, who has since gone off to other pastures. (Not currently a matter of furor, what she wears or how her hair is done; if it were, the reaction of some of us, clinging as we do day after day to the dismembered planks of a life raft, would be strictly unprintable.)

The cultural furniture, the atmosphere, are a kind of sterile Scandinavian transplant, reassembled here with domestic glues and fabrics.

But it is the last page of the *Life* spread that gave me pause. A double page is given over to a close-up of the three returned men, grinning behind the glass wall of their decontamination cage. Opposite, the text of a poem by James Dickey. The poem, and its implications, are perhaps worth a pause in the day's occupations, as another poet put it long ago.

John, our guru, quoted above and elsewhere in this work, was writing with the lucidity of the true visionary. Object: to comprehend the world and to surpass it, in the very act.

Dickey, also a poet, lingers in a kind of heavy-breathing incantatory style, around the particular and funky items which make up the grab bag of earth and moon. Of course, the poet must be aware to his fingertips of this, that, everything; choosey as an old pensioner in a flea market.

But one must not be entirely satisfied with a sense of the world, a sense of the moon. The question is legitimate; what did the poet bring home—junk or sustenance?

The verdict on the poem charges, junk. The leap for mankind ends, artistically speaking, in another pothole.

Question: do the poet or his patrons wish us to disencumber ourselves, in the old Greek sense, to purge ourselves? Was there an imaginative victory in the poem, in the sense that it introduced the truth on an untruthful scene? One is allowed to wonder.

One is allowed to question. Such questioning being outside the ken of Mitchell or Agnew or Nixon—or indeed of Mailer or Dickey;

    that edgy task of the intelligence, the "feel of things,"
      the hands,
      the shoulders unburdened
        with the heavy chain and its medallion
        inscribed; Court Historian;
          or, The Truth, Official Version.

I was in New England, at a conference on Violence in America, during the Apollo landings. Ours was yet another try at understanding; The Whole Schtick, Where It Is Going. In attendance we had a rigid State Department man, a less rigid Justice Department man (better steel in State), an older generation radical, a concerned sociologist, a third-world scholar, a black intellectual, a middle-road middle ager with modest political aspirations, and two black cops from (God help them) the Chicago police force. And myself; by advertisement, a religious resister— a sport, biologically speaking.

Certain members of this unlikely team (you may guess who), in the time between rounds, hung over the TV set like damp laundry, heads and feet attached. Our boys were landing, walking, setting up the flag, on schedule.

There was, as one may judge, a conflict of interest among us. Several mutually unassimilable visions of life, time, man, God, history, whatever. Oil was oil; water, water.

I would conclude in retrospect that we added considerably to the quantum of violence which was to be our subject, but not our object. So hot did things get, in fact, that the conference hardly held together at all; marred by apoplectic departures, sustained only by the patience of a core group and by last-minute arrivals, timed to get in a few punches and run.

From a year's perspective, the event has a certain humorous aspect; in fact, it was a horror on both sides. For me, wandering the earth under appeal for assorted federal felonies, it was a last hurrah of sorts, shouted in the baffled faces of presumed opposite numbers.

Pursuant to all of which
        I am led to Mr. Dickey's poem,
which accompanies as a kind of choral ode, the
    three faces
        of the triumphant repatriates
                their moon lode their lore and lure
                                and glory.
Now it is obvious that in the space afforded a poet by
                        LIFE
        one cannot say everything cannot invoke every
        voice of a given event.
                I am not asking Dickey to hide in priest
                                holes
    like the last member of an all but extinguished
                                species
        to harken to presences audible in the dark
while fellow Americans range and raven the outer
                    reaches of available empire.
No, I am a man rendered simple by adversity
        a poet also
                questioning after the example of John of
                                the Cross
        truth and illusion, reality and its apes
        a moralist if you will. The occasion offered,
                I would invite Dickey
            to taste my recent menu; Chomsky, Zinn,
Goodman, Jefferson, Lincoln, Cleaver
            to recoil like a scalded man under the let
                                blood
        of blacks reds browns yellows whites

111

to allow to fall upon his hovering pen   his cunning muse
the shadows of copters over Berkeley   guns over
Carolina
To take into account and compassion
what men suffer who bear the heavy and main
weight
of portages over the polluted stream of events
the days that fall   a slow dynamited wall
upon the lives of brothers   our brothers.
But to the poem. Dickey says(I presume he speaks
in the *persona*
of the 3 space men)
"We are here to do one
Thing only and that is rock by rock to carry the
moon to take it
Back."
Which is bad poetry. Not because of this or that
in detail or style
but because it betrays the truth of consciousness.
Because it celebrates and approves a childish venture and offers us
no "relief from outside."
Probably against all intent of evil
(Americans never intend evil)
it links three space innocents to the
innocent activity
of crusaders, Cortez, puritans, Kit Carson,
southerners,
northerners, marines, US expeditionary forces, the
US air force,

the piscine marauder I saw issuing like a shark from
its nest in New London, Conn., last July
a nuclear sub   loaded with eggs   spoiling for birth
making conditionally
for some unconditional showdown in whatever
waters.

A reviewer of my last book wrote, expressing his
reservations about Catonsville
and anticipating our answer;
"You do not have to propose an alternative, to
know an omelette is stinking."
So be it. Let our friends join us this far; let
them cry,
the omelette is stinking. Indeed, the
stink,
which we have not caused, may be of the
substance of truth.
It may be a kind of saving heroism, to
turn in a 360-degree arc
eyes open,   where one stands   and say
aloud
I wonder why there are no more hummingbirds in
this area?
or say aloud, in the words of John;
The understanding should not feed upon
visions.
Or to stand upon a roof of west side Man-
hattan and cry;
No one in the city has seen a passage of migratory
fowl for years and years.

113

Mr. Dickey, whose lines celebrate the grabbing
of moon rocks
off the moon scape
takes no note of such absences   nor does
he incorporate them
in his prospectus of survivals, arrivals, et al.
So much for the despised and public function of
poetry.
But some of us
hearkening to the sound of buckshot announc-
ing legally   promptly
the extinction of pink herons   white foxes
black panthers
and other dispensable fauna
shake in our main bones and fibres   not
altogether altruistically.

It is the night of April 17, toward morning. I set this
down; somewhere in the folds and pockets of my mind
is a folded paper, a single scrawled word. And I pose the
question, as a matter of public interest: Who's next? I
invite all those who lie under similar menace, to undertake
a like predawn exercise
to that whiff of dawn wind that chills
all natural warmth.
The understanding should not feed upon
visions.

The Understanding Should Not Feed upon Visions Continued. The Subject Being of Some Import to the Denizens of These 50 States, the Discussion Continues, in Somewhat the Following Form. The Shade of Our Guru Is Summoned.

Friend: But then what should it feed on? itself? its own guts, like the boy carrying the fox in the legend?
John: No. On reality.
Friend: Reality, of course. But you are removing utopia, paradise, tomorrow, all those hints and starts and senses of things that make today bearable and tomorrow possible, removing them from the field of vision. My eye needs them; and I say why not?
John: (smiling) You tend to forget; I am something of a

visionary myself. But I forbid the soul to traffic in whatever weakens the soul. Maybe—

F: (explodes) You have no sense of what we are going through! Did you hear of the latest self-immolation? (He opens the May 19 paper) And a letter from a dead GI condemning the war; he left the letter to be opened in event of his death. He requested "a civilian burial." And Mitchell visits the campus where two black students were killed last week, and reports: "very useful meetings, in view of similar incidents which may occur in the future." And you object to our holding to some vision or other? You ought to be marveling at our ability to stay sane!

J: "Some vision or other." Exactly the point. Some visions are rotten and rot the mind which contains them. Did you ever reflect, for example, that the Attorney General too is ruled somberly by a vision? and the Pentagon also?

F: But these are not ours! Ours are far from these as night from day! Listen, every day brings such a dose of bad news, such a windfall of rotten fruit and dead branches down on our heads; do you wonder that we create some sort of world to crawl into and survive?

J: What is it like? Tell me.

F: It has to do with human relationships, human decency, the free play of love and life, spontaneity, joy even. We abhor cocktails and bombs and the dead decision makers gathering to carve up the world, to decree who shall survive and who die, and for what.

J: This is no way to argue. You're describing, in somewhat rhapsodic terms, no more than the common legacy of men. Who doesn't want these things? Who wouldn't concede that not to want them is not to be a man at all? The question has to go deeper; so deep in fact that it drowns the foolhardies who venture out . . .

F: But if you're willing to suffer and even to die; if you're willing to put off your personal well-being and embrace that of another, if—if you don't give a nickel about all the items of the luxury lists you were supposed to check off, one by one, as signs you had made it—

J: One presupposes all that. In bad times, unusual men are the only ones worth talking to, worth beginning with. So you are altruistic, unselfish, passionate about the crimes of silence, of power, of connivers? Let me thank you and pat you on the head; and let's get on please with the real issues . . .

F: You define them then.

J: Something like this: every flag has its pole, every kite its string. Who sends up what sorts of signs? Signs of what? Life, death, possession, clairvoyance, fear, despair, community? Almost everyone engaged in kiteflying is watching the kites; that's the game. But who follows the string downward says: I wonder what those people are like, those beautiful people, gassed by their own game.

F: Your metaphor's easier with the flag. Everyone I know turns away from the house or factory or porch or car that carries the plague sign.

J: Turns away no doubt. But who seeks to understand? or grows in self understanding? and in turning away, what does one turn to? . . . Tell me, do you ever meditate?

F: Yes, when the spirit moves me.

J: Why?

117

F: Why does one breathe? What are eyes for? The question makes no sense. On the river yesterday, I saw a flock of wild ducks come down. They swam and fed for a while on the waters; some of them rested, closed their eyes, floated there. They lingered almost as long as I. And I thanked them: you've come almost as far as I have, and there's all heaven's spaces ahead. They took off again, heavily, as though on some signal, grave and disciplined, like philosophers changed into birds. Everything they did there, I was doing. I was with them; where they came from, where they were going, all they were about. What I did was pray. It seemed as though my spirit had been granted access to theirs.

J: What else have you done this week?

F: The usual. Strike on Monday, draft board demonstration on Tuesday (arrest and release, the predictable charade); work at the Press on Wednesday; grass party in the evening. Battles with parents, *passim.* Try to avoid, try to live with, the latest catastrophe out of Washington. Try to stay sane. Try to make it, for one more day. So used not to making it, used to being cut down to size, most of the time one feels either decapitated or cut off at the knees . . .

But you've been asking all the questions. Let me try a few . . . That book of yours now. What does it have to say to me; all that God talk. You know we mistrust it; it it comes out of flannelmouths and goes in plaster ears . . . My parents are fervent churchgoers.

J: That book. It could disappear tomorrow and hardly a librarian know the difference; let alone you—or me, for that matter. What really counts is that you came on it. It got us moving toward one another, got us talking.

F: They say you're a saint. What does that mean?

J: Let's say, a private man with a public reach.

F: Translate?

J: I had no money; so there was nothing to buy or sell. As though the world were a great flea market, with the price tags off, and no haggling allowed. I also very nearly died of hunger, thirst, cold, heat, ague, plague, malice and loveless-ness. Not to speak of the zeal of fanatics, who thought to purify the room by removing the occupant; permanently.

F: But what did you believe in? Did you fight for anything?

J: I fought like a demon for my own soul—against demons. You see only the finished product, after time has set up the ikon or the presses have turned out the book. But if you could touch my hand, like this (he reaches out his hand), and hear my voice; or better, if you could have gone with me on that dusty bloody round; from filthy jail to torrid roads, from hideout to court room and back again—that would have helped!

F: How did you make it, how did you stay with it?

J: There was nothing else to be done. There was a question to be dealt with, the text was like a hieroglyphic scrawled with a stick in the mud and dust; how will the next genera-tion live? I had to pursue it, to its last letter, memorizing, improvising, speculating as I went. And when I reached the end, I was full of days and journeys and beatings and prisons and horrors—and God. I was stuffed like a capon, like Dives. I died, heavy with those delicacies, curled up like a child around the last letter of that lifelong text,

drinking it all in. I dreamed I died with a smile on my lips.
F: But you lived by a vision. And died for it. And yet you cast doubt on mine.
J: Every vision ought to have doubt cast on it, to keep it visionary. Otherwise we end up with flags and messiahs—and murder. The old game all over again; nothing accomplished for human beings. Don't you ever have doubts about your life, your friends, your acts?
F: Weren't you ever young? If you were, even for a day, you wouldn't ask something like that.
J: And yet you want to be certified; prime beef, grade-A eggs, *haute cuisine* omelette.
F: I want—enough light to make it by.
J: How much light is that? If you're nearly blind, obviously a great deal. Bats and cats and moles get further with less.
F: They aren't so condemned to being Americans.
J: They aren't condemned to being human. That's the rub; that's also the determinant of light and its measure. You want a de luxe quantum; you need glasses, you need high voltage. You need God: switch, operator, watt dispenser, a top executive, Consolidated Edison, owner of the gasworks.
F: Now you're being idiotic; not to say offensive. Anyone who's been around one graveyard, one ghetto, one university, one suburban home, one head or freak or resister knows what we need. We need what we don't have. We need what's been stolen from us. We need what the rapists of power have searched out and destroyed, strangled and buried in secret. We need God and man.
J: Yes. That's in fact what we started with, what the power-

ful can never start with. Why they never start at all. And why when push comes to shove, they can toil like Sisyphus and never move us—because it's all uphill. We have sewn into our skins the ballast, the inertia of history itself. And the landscape leans over, lends itself to us, in love.

But our conflict remains, a matter of love; a serious matter. You said you required God and man and light and all sorts of other goods and services. Your catalogue sounds a little like the Ecological Needs of an Orchid Compiled in a Fifth Avenue Penthouse. Maybe we can change the question. What do you have to give?

F: To give? Visions.

J: Visions. Do they have blood on them?

Being a Suggested Beginners' List of Visions the Mind Should Not Feed Upon.

The subject continues to be proposed. This may be thought strange by those whose inner ocular equipment has never rested upon the kingdoms of this world, or of that.

For others, the crystalline enticement is a real and present danger. They know that man is dealt with in very different ways by time and this world—both racked and raised above—destroyed piecemeal, rendered weightless.

We speak of the good man, whose effort to make the world inhabitable by men, and men inhabitable by one another, sets loose against him the ferocious rage of those who are asked to make room for reality, truth, compassion. One must hasten to add: the term "beast" applied to human conduct is used analogously. There is no direct way

122

I know of, to convey the instinctual actions of man, confronted by the nervous, exposed, vulnerable goodness of his fellow: We do the world of animals an outrageous injustice in substituting those for these. Hunters, trappers, dealers in pelts and feathers, owners of abattoirs, ladies clothed in the furs of small, exotic, nearly extinct animals—these often know the world of beasts not at all; that is to say, only in useful edible marketable ways (dead) or fighting tooth, claw and eye, the onslaught of death. Therefore ungrateful and unresponsive, untamable. Who, they seem to be asking in the very spasm of their extremity, who would be housebroken to you, a broken house? The good man: an apt pupil for the inhabitive spirits, for the destroyers and undoers, as well as the teachers and lovers. To be Freudian or Jungian is not necessarily to be adequate to our subject. Yet again, the data of analogies may be of help. It seems to me that, almost humorously—certainly in good humor, we are striving to define according to certain very obscure criteria, the man of health, the sane man. He is, like a miraculous tropical fish, in motion while we observe him, attempt to get to know him. Indeed he has little interest in our project; any more than a fish, one was tempted to say. Or like a fish, he must be persuaded, preferably by another of his own species, that a project or proposition makes sense.

According to our guru, such a man is also infested by the spirits; he will never be rid of them; his house is haunted. He is in principle, stuck; his life is of devastating interest to a mysterious world of heroic and subhuman spirits. They make of him their sounding board; their infinitely suggestive power vibrates around him. They wish to know, by

123

the influence they can wield over him, what outcome their own existence bears. Thus, in the words of Sartre, they attempt to set up serious dialogue with man, then to interiorize the dialogue, and finally to make their voices indistinguishable from his own. In the resulting condition —call it confusion, temptation, possession—a certain victory has been won (or lost); a man has become, in the process of living, a different man, in a sense both shockingly discernible and bafflingly obscure.

Now is this to be considered as merely a "way of speaking," drawn from outmoded religion by eminent crackpots, to gain control of public funds, in order to build more and better belfries for bats?

In the matter under discussion, some measure of knowledge of the mind and its functions is undoubtedly of help. This is all the more important, since very few specialists have chosen to take seriously the questions opened by these pages; the new man, the healthy man, the revolutionary ethos, freedom, change. Laing, Cooper, Coles, Erikson, Goodman, Dennison, Marcuse, each in his way, have tried to open these questions; sanity, insanity, the relations of each to the structures of man, to his wars, his loves, his literature, his cities. Beyond these, though, there is very little.

In dead disciplines, there are no caucuses. Are the psychiatric arts and sciences, and their practitioners, dead to all change, all access beyond the most limited—and limiting? Their heavy center, located somewhere in the turtle's guts, lumbers along; it carries its furniture, its justification, and sets the direction and pace. Who will knock upon the case, with the code, the news? . . .

But in any case, to our vision; not to be entertained, by hypothesis.

Let us for modest beginning, round up with nets, narcoticizing blowguns and merciful sprays, a few CHOICE HUMAN SPECIMENS, men, women and children. Let them be transported, even against their will, from distant points like S.E. Asia, to our continental midst. Or after a modest "incursion" here, from among our own eagerly spawning masses. Let the subjects be properly deloused, dewormed, given such medical, dental, psychiatric and religious attention as they may be supposed to require. Then let them be lodged in an artful urban center, accoutred with reasonable comforts, adapted according to a model of an ideal zoo.

Let us admit for a start, that such a project is visionary, in the sense that it is ahead of the times. It would undoubtedly excite, for a brief time, the fury of a small segment of the populace. Not for long! One must be confident, in the light of human adaptive power; headlines would shrink in size and detonation, to back pages, then float gently off the public consciousness, bombarded as it is with distraction and frenzied with private burdens, their stench, the albatrosses of successive crisis.

No, we have nothing to fear, save fear itself. The question, in spite of all who would defame or disclaim, remains: Is it worth our while to have under constant scientific and popular scrutiny (a glass house; visible in, opaque out) as to habits of breeding, feeding, converse, rhythms and relations, a segment of the abundant human fauna, translated from its primitive or decadent ambiance, or our own?

(Those whose moral fury is presently expended on the extinctive methods of war, might be defused by the suggestion, it is surely better, more morally persuasive, to save a few than to level the whole.) We are proposing in fact nothing more startling than a modern adaptation of an old event. In colonial times, exemplary members of dusky or saffron or copper-skinned savages, were borne from their bush and temples, to the palaces of Western kings. There, they stirred the courts with their exotic splendor, their spontaneous untranslatable gutturals and labials.

More practically. We are in trouble. We are afflicted with a vast measure of perplexity about our future. In a manner of speaking, we stumble and nearly fall in the potholes of our cities, the hidden nests and hideouts of our nuclear defense. We breathe shallowly our slovenly air. The fish flip belly up in our murky waters, a portent. We have need of a certain effort of imagination; to construct areas which are off-limits to a creeping plague; to guard those limits as we guard the animals of Asia and the tropics; to hold under loving detention, in protective custody, seed banks, brain banks, emotion banks, a variety of upright, thinking *sapientes*, objects of a wide-sweeping pacification. Inevitable, the duress of immediate moral hazard must be met. There are shades lurking to whisper their obdurate prohibition against the long term, stubbornly obscure GREATER GOOD. We must oppose such voices, and move on with our project. In no other way, I hazard, shall we come upon a hint of the future; that future so assiduously obscured from the most determined and delicate instrumentality. Ha!

126

And Finally a Few Visions Which It Is Lawful Nay Laudable to Entertain

It would seem, at first blush, that a visionary has no right forbidding men their visions. (The first blush is usually the correct one.) Except, as the preceding has attempted to show, such visions as are rank, deceptive, downright foolish, or whose entertainment (in the form of recurrent fantasy) results in harmful treatment of animals, small children, the natural world.

On this principle, into the trash can must be relegated, with whatever regret, nearly all the Rest and Recreation poolside ruminations of generals, together with the conversations that, poured into gold-plated phones, charm the shell-like ear of Greek oil heiresses. As well as the hatred of small minds, aroused by the rare emergence of one or another black family from its shacktown, gaining a room or so, a window or so, a tree or so, under the inflamed territoriality of white spies and wardens. One could go on. The list is distressingly large. Perhaps it is time, though, to take what steps we can, from encompassing darkness into rare light, to show what visions might be of some account, where paradise might be located, planned and planted. Let us try.

Paradise Park. For the people, not for the kings. In fact, excised from their boundless holding. If possible, the acres should be "granted" the people, in a legal writ, with public fanfare, reminiscent of the opening of western abundance. A land grant, after the land grabs have frozen the market and lowered the shades, in the possibility of open vistas for the festering, foreshortened gaze of millions of our children. (Such an idea will be met with some indignation. Many of us being at some remove from the facts here adduced, never having seen a child who has never seen a cow, a sheep, or a clear running stream.)

A certain defined, abundant space therefore, bearing along its humans, into the variety of waters, valleys, flowering trees, the landscape transposed to our fading dreams, from afar, our impoverished distance from its actuality . . .

In such a park, moreover, let approved conduct and policy fall away with the clank of struck chains. People sit down before the spreading napkin of the universe. They neither sow nor reap nor weep in secret nor get arrested nor barter in inferior foodstuffs nor bicker in despair nor reside in gross and hateful proximity to rodents and roaches. The "business" of living, which for most of them is a dolorous rehearsal for dying, is suspended. Or indeed, to explore our metaphor, here the living are granted at least equal rights with the dead; the supposition being that living bodies need to wander, loiter, maunder—at least as much as ghosts do.

Let us turn over this bright coin of our fancy, and scrub away the tarnish which neglect, cowardice or cupidity have allowed to gather there. In our park there shall be no cop, mortician, scalper, pusher, truant officer, real-estate developer, sociologist, academic Peeping Tom, religious-tract distributor, do-gooder or do-badder—to none of these should admission be granted. Or if they wish to enter, let them be stripped of all exercise of their gruesome rites. But no hustling here. Let us have a free zone, laughter, released stays and buttons and zippers, a few lovers or many. Let the people enter, grow, run, fly, perambulate, consume, pull corks from, spread jams and peanut butter on, swim and sun in, et cetera as the day is long. . . .

A vision about animals. Leon Bloy, no mean visionary, thought they were a clue to paradise. The clue, let it be said, has never even been discovered by most, let alone pondered or decoded. No, in our usual dreams, we shrink from violent teeth and claws, our heroes destroy the polluted dragons, our dark forests are plagued with vermin, the cries of daws, infestations of bats and Draculas. Human metamorphoses are loaded in our favor:

The stories go according to pattern. That is to say, the animals are never heard from. A man, sometimes lying under a curse, is changed dreadfully in frame and soul: to a beetle, a ravening bear, or a simple tree. The stories almost never pursue the question whether the changeling is capable of the decent, lucid, exemplary conduct of those maligned beings. My impression is that, almost invariably, such fictions and transmutations malign the true form of the world and place animals at a hopeless disadvantage; a kind of perpetual prejudice of guilt, resulting often enough in their being placed under "preventive custodial care" or hunted down with vigor. (Cf. the history of the original black panther, extant almost totally through the art of taxidermy.)

Thus our dreams are in the nature of unexamined (or misinterpreted) emanations from the steamy recess of history, crime, inner turmoil, vagrant impulse. They should, I would think, be regarded strictly as our own creation, the tricky embodiment of ignorance and desire—and laziness of spirit. To suppose, on the other hand, that they grant us clues to the conduct of the creatures of this world is, to say the least, a gratuitous one.

One must be hopeful, none the less. It may be that we are nearing the end of that long cycle which condemns the snake to bear the burden of all our ills; tail, sinuous length, and tongue. A most patient beast, to bear so gracefully the cries, sticks and stones of such relentless pursuit. Almost the Jew of the ruined kingdom.

I would rather start again; a Franciscan movement. Its emblem is a painting by Blake or Rousseau, of naked lovers. (A. and E. were lovers, we forget, before they cried sour grapes upon the world.) They are surrounded by a very congress of glad day creatures, with whom they are in communion and play; the very creatures who by a miracle of benevolence and diuturnity, still wander in some places and fly in some skies . . .

I know a city that glories in its marvelous zoo. The animals seem, not so much content (a value judgment; they have no vote in the matter) as resigned. They inhabit a reasonable acreage, so contrived as to give them some taste of their origins, and a semblance of freedom.

In the same city, the municipal jail is a matchbox horror, inflammable and spiritually dampening at once. The prisoners, it is said, would gladly enter negotiations with the animals for an exchange of facilities. Even, it is said, for one day a month; preferably in summer. But the experience of the animals at the hands of humans has rendered them as wary as American Indian braves. They show little or no interest.

A kind of cold comfort is born. In at least one of our cities, the animals are more mercifully housed and more carefully nourished, than a sizable number of humans. (What this might mean, given the current direction of public policy, I leave to experts.) Some facts are clear, and hint at the direction of things. In cold-cash terms, it comes to this. Human beings are of less worth than those burnished pelts, those iridescent plumes, those roarers and songsters and hoofs and claws. Moreover, men are multiplying; the common estimate of individual worth is, in consequence, shrinking. And this, while many species of beasts and birds are dying out.

The consumer body politic, firmly bound about with its

money belt, a sacred torrid zone, plays out its game of truth and consequence.

To wit. Creation is assembled like a vast slave market before these omnipotent speculators, buyers and sellers. In general, as the trading goes, animals fetch better prices than men, animals are hauled off in better conveyances, to more humane fates. I kid you not. It is coming, it has already come.

(The above has ended otherwise than I intended; a vision that is to be "entertained" not for its entertainment value, but because it is a strict supposition for survival. The kind of road map once offered through haunted forests by fairy godmothers, to untried boys and girls.)

Boys and girls in such tales often ended up dead, covered by the birds of the air with a pall of leaves. These are the sad facts of the world; consult your road map frequently; and in desolate areas, check your gas meter before venturing.

I ventured out this morning into my neighborhood, which is uninfested, as far as I can judge. I saw a barelegged old lady, bent over, pruning her sparse flowers with a tool. Her blue-veined legs were firmly planted; her white hair was alight in the sun. The innocence of the scene! I wished that she might survive.

I Am Not Even Sure That the Following Is a Visionary Statement: Decide Please for Yourself

Jesus says;
Do not let your left hand know   what your right hand is doing
Are we considering here   a mere counsel of prudence
such as would govern say the
    surreptitious schizoid life   of a devout public servant
his Sunday hand dispensing
    goodies to God   his weekday hand lively as Fagin's in and
                                          out of the public till

his face golden as a buttercup   a buttermilk cow   in whose mouth forsooth
                butter would not melt

No I would think of something   more serious
first of the deliberate blindness   imposed by Jesus on doers of good works
                                      so that they become in a sense adept at

                yin   yang
the rhythm of light   and dark
    lucidity   ignorance
    rightful pride   self abasement   we might say maturity

133

sufficient to regard the
        unfinished world
    its cauldron of suffering
summoning other fools
with curious bright lust
the cry that rises from their marrow

The words apply I submit to visionary
                                man

'as my two eyes make one in sight'
hold in two cupped hands
the bird about to fly
        the untried burden
Present and future!
is to grant it full bloom
        To release the bird

In this sense I judge

and refrain from the fool's cockadoodledoo
to run to taste   that bloody broth
upon the plight of those dismembered bones
.
which was once man

ambidexterous   so to speak   in eye
so does such a man .
the hardly open flower   the future
upon whose untried wings rests
of future air
to breathe upon the flower

is to grant it
its proper telos   freedom
the saying is visionary   and correct

functional to man

he both gardens that flower

the bird returns to him

Thus every paradise   root and
flower   is both untouchable
mystery

Make it happen!

bringing together   as the task
of a lifetime   gradually patiently
or both of these   commingled
Their gesture   a consummation
the hands of Jesus while
time endures wide apart the forced wracking
the hands of Buddha
the distance between them measuring

whose frame and spirit   are so cunningly
conjoined
and wears it   his proper perfection and
ornament
vatic   miraculous   in its beak a sprig of
green   from unknown soil

and present possession   I do not know how
else to say it   except to urge
ignorance and wisdom   light and the unknown

an infolding of tragic or coming intent
those two hands of his
We must strictly imagine

of the cross   alienation   anomie   agony
more gently disposed   resting apart

the millennial patience   of that lotus
bud and bloom

It Seems Expedient to Return to the Words of Our Guru Here Appended Together with Certain Comments (Which Later May Be Ignored at Will)

> The soul of man must be emptied
> of all imagined forms   figures   and   images
> and must remain in darkness
> if it is to attain to divine union

Such a statement is almost a commonplace with John; it is good to recall it, if only because he places such stress upon it. Many ask how to meditate, as though to do so were merely to take in hand some valued document, the Gospel, the sayings of this or that guru; to cherish the words, and give attention to them. But we perhaps do not realize that according to classical teaching of all the masters, in so acting, one lingers around a mere preliminary, perhaps persuaded that it is the main matter. "The eyes of the master (in an old saying) are the way to his heart." Exactly. Do not neglect the heart, attending only to the direction of his gaze. Every way out is, finally, a way in. But the way is by a steady attentive welcoming of darkness; the way of unknowing. I leave it to you, how neatly this flips over the usual theory, so alive in the blood of actionists, on "getting somewhere"; whether to the moon, or to the fiber of things.

> Just so the steps of a staircase
>   are merely the means to reach the room
> to which it leads.
> If the man climbing the stairs
> would linger on any one of them
> he would never arrive
> So the man who is to attain to union
> must pass through   leave behind
> all meditations   forms   apprehensions
> for they bear no resemblance or proportion
> to God

The words, it seems to me, contain much good sense, are so lucid as to make comment an intrusive act. The image of a staircase, maybe by implication, either a nightmare rather or a vision. The stairs "make sense" when they lift man, in gradual conquest of gravity, to some new level of things. When they wind and twist forever, they become a horror, as dreams show us, in the common life of the psyche. No, there is a door at the top, and a room; in a literal and yet teasing sense, there will be room

there; for friends, for leveling off, for an end to the climb.
Unknown and yet inviting. Other voices, seasons, vistas.
The future? Nourishment? a table is spread there.

> At a certain point
> man no longer enjoys
> that food of sense
> He needs another kind of food   more delicate
> more internal
> a food which imparts to his soul
> deep quietude and repose of spirit

Two sorts of menus are necessary to man. (Well, all
sorts; let us be arbitrary.) The one enables him to climb
the stairs; his workaday menu taken in haste perhaps, with
an eye to the long climb ahead. The last meal of the
Hebrews in Egypt is instructive; they had to eat standing,
as a sign of extreme haste, the crisis of getting out of
bondage alive. It would have been foolish and improvi-
dent to depart fasting (the journey would endure for some
forty years). On the other hand, it would have been supreme foolishness to risk everything by relaxing, cooking,
consuming a banquet. What point could there be in cele-
brating? Their spirit was filled with foreboding and awe
and more than a just measure of fear. So they ate in haste,
on foot, stuff in hand, accoutred for a journey. Ah, but
the arrival! that was so momentous an event, the menu
for its marking had been hinted at all along the way,
odors and tastes that bordered on the miraculous. They
ate manna from heaven; and when they neared the land
of promise, their scouts returned, loaded with fabulous
fruits; to the parched and weary people, bearing the very
fruits of paradise . . .

They settled finally on the land and sat to banquet; the occasion was primordial and unending; it was a sealing of the promise, a fateful hour which stretched out to include and fold in upon all the future. They would never cease to arrive, they would never cease to celebrate! That table spread forward to eternity; time unrolled like a banquet cloth. No more steps to be taken; no more days on the road, nights in bivouac, only continuing joy, arrival, consummation, the task of celebration. The fruits of time, their sour and sweet delights, were the liberal foretaste of eternity.

It is of this John speaks. The banquet is a figure of contemplation. The contemplation is the banquet, forever savored, tasted again, assimilated, interiorized. The menu has no "efficiency" to it; no reason beyond itself, except to lend delight to the heart of man. Taste and see!

> The more a man learns to abide in the spirit
> the more his particular acts
> come to a halt
> since his soul
> comes more and more to unity
> in one undivided and pure act
> So a man ceases his labor
> even as his feet cease to move
> and come to a halt
> when his journey is ended

The image is closely related to the last passage; when the exodus is over, men sit down. But not just to anything, not just anywhere; the sign of the end of the journey, the emblem of its transcendent meaning, is the banquet it gives rise to. That incomparable menu!

Otherwise a directionless journey. You have seen people on such a treadmill; they confess it to friends, in tears and despair. Or the image of the seemingly powerful, purposeful drum of great autos on a highway. Speed, safety, sense!

Well, maybe.

You must look at the faces, even in the plastic repose of those orange-roofed oases, where purportedly, the tribe that pauses, refreshes. They often seem in fact, like people released from some universal squeeze play, their juices wrung dry, their lives catapulted fearsomely down highways, end over end in sealed tin cans, down and up and down again; brinksmanship, the dangerous pleasure of rolling over Niagara in a sealed barrel, seized on, technologized, common as a mill run. Some, it is variously reported, do not make the falls; they perish before the next orange rest room. But if it is dangerous to be alive at all, who quails before the bloody percentages?

I sense it simply, the guru opens another vista. The feet of man, those good carriers, are also to know repose. Treadmills, squirrel cages, are not, for all their ubiquity, apt figures of the universe. Slow down, slow down.

You have seen loads of those flattened car bodies, being dragged off to the pachyderm's graveyard on truck trailers, a load of ivory and bones borne by a living elephant. To bury dead slaves, we requisition the living, as slaves. Thus the cycle. But how to break it? You break it by refusal. Refusal of the distraught, distempered, misbegotten out of hand, out of mind, dis-order of things. In that surreal demonic nether world, oil discovers Alaska, nightmares have men, war is peace, and grabs are up for you and me. The password is not, watch out! but, watch in!

140

Only a Guru Would Have Dared Write It: "The Benefits Which Arise from Forgetfulness." We Will, at His Behest, Pursue the Subject.

Remember—v. To recall by an act or effort of memory.
Re-member—v. To put together a living thing.
Forget—v. To cease to recall or remember (e.g.) one's name; amnesia.

A son who cannot (will not?) remember his father. Fathers who forget their sons, out of wrath or neglected or despised hopes.

The amnesiac nation; inability literally, vitally, to grasp the forward moving implications of its own beginning—i.e., to give numbers of people simply a decent chance in the world. To relieve burdens, to offer hope to the despairing. A kind of Isaiah message at the foot of Liberty.

141

Is amnesia due to imperialistic parasitic growth on consciousness—or to the impurity of the beginning itself? Most Americans would find the words of their Constitution and Declaration, intolerable. What has gone wrong?

Radical loss of memory, that tool of the "continuum of action"; the loss aided and abetted by amnesiac religion. Come, let us forget together. "Blessed are the peacemakers" perverted in practice, to its exact antonym—a blessing on war.

Radical amnesia in the individual, thus compounded.

Consider the case of a young citizen, grown uneasy under orders of the state, turning to the Church for an enlightened memory, a radical ikon, a resource of spirit . . . A word of Jesus, strongly spoken in the face of Caesar's wrath.

(Or Pirandello's King Henry: an amnesiac in a world like a barred madhouse; the king purportedly has lost all continuity of memory; he recalls neither the accident which damaged his mind, nor events of a ear ago, nor of an hour ago. But what of the world? Henry's mad craft suggests that it is all of a piece . . . he is no madder than his subjects or keepers. . . .)

Our citizen friend turns, this way and that, seeking sane relief; let us admit; he is modest; he is seeking some echo of the voice of Jesus in that chamber of history where, it is claimed, the voice of Jesus vibrates endlessly, as in a coiled shell; better, since the claim is no mere echo, a sibyl's cave.

Alas. He enters a second chamber of the unconscious. The Church has forgotten. She literally does not know what he is talking about. Bad history does not lacerate her mind as it did the mind of her master; a thorn, a bleeding passionate spur, the iron spur of that cock Peter heard, raking the brain, urging alternatives, urging—life? let us say, revealing literally, in the evidence of blood, the cost of change.

Such is an old church, like an old king, like an old general, like an old parent—a source of fretful despair (so he concludes). They all talk the same. You can't get beyond those filmy eyes. They have never been raked by the cock's razor spur, heard his brassy Olly-olly-ox-in-freee! signifying the end of the game, end of war; all in free and safe!

Jesus; the easiest one in all history to forget; not merely to forget, to turn on. To condemn again. The question is not about Hitler; it concerns grand inquisitors; churchmen. "He had to go; he was impeding the real show, which is keeping people moral, keeping them in line . . ." And by "people" I don't of course mean kings (even mad kings or mad generals). Churchmen are drawn to Locke, who said, It's perfectly correct to herd, feed, and generally control the masses, until they get to the point where they can take over their own care, housebreaking, table manners. An arrogant sort, who saw history like the frozen landscape of a zoo, animals (people) hibernating, only the guards about checking the trees, infested with sleeping bears and bees, the foxholes full of believers . . .

NB. When things are bad, everyone tends to act like everyone else. All the delight and interplay of temperament, talent, ignorance, funkiness, black and gray and white humor, edge of mind—these get lost, like the contents of a home swept into a tornado. What's left? a shell, everyone transformed, transfixed by fear, into suicidal self-destroyers.

I even offer a law of sorts, deduced from experience. 1) It is a tactic of bad power to make public conditions seem worse than they are to create worse news for bad; 2) When the panic announcement takes hold, we can trust amnesia to take over; the danger signal burns so brightly, it draws energy and fuel from all other conduits; men burn with a single flame. Usually hatred, fear, vengefulness; 3) Single words, phrases, tend to compel human conduct into the desired direction; even judgmental, cool minds, become tinder for the awaited conflagration. (Orwell's five-minute Hate, induced solely by the televised photo of The Enemy.) 4) It would be a very nampurna of foolishness to think the Church could be immunized against such transmutations of language or method. Hell no. She too hears what Socrates spoke of, the skill of making and keeping false peace, of "making the worse appear the better cause . . ."

Sometimes imperialism is so obviously a church project, we tend to think of her as simply an adjunct to the throne. She plans crusades, builds fleets, swaps heavenly real estate, trades her credentials of heavenly favor, for Caesar's.

Today we've democratized the thing. Keep the forces distinct (abstractly distinct). The gentleman's agreement, (usually visible first of all to the losers), means that the war (any war, let's be big) can go on, with the implicit blessing of Church on state. In a state as ridden with bad religion as ours, as shot through with the protestations of faith in God, mother, and flag uttered throughout seamy history by land-grabbers, robber barons, ward bosses, cardinals, speculators, strikebreakers, from snake-oil peddler's wagons, to presidential podiums—well, quite a formidable thing! What, in all heaven or hell, is our young unspoiled, troubled citizen to think? Where is he to go for radical aid to right memory? Who is to help him recall the vow of his youth—that he would be a man, that he would deal with other men in decency and truth?

Stranger in a strange land. Fly in spider web, unwilling visitant; better split, he thinks; is so right.

He is accused of being alienated, of breaking off connections, of refusing to join a community ready, before him, wanting him. That look on the faces of parents when the good they have labored over, is trespassed, vaulted over. . . .

That loss. To both sides. Amnesia inducing alienation. Not so simple a matter as turning aside from manifest evil, something infinitely more complex; the bloodletting struggle that goes on in the midst of good things, that somehow are not good enough, their implication or privilege and wrong power . . .

In bad times, everyone tends to take the same instinctive action, to speak a like language, to wear the same faces. Then, the protest: they all look alike to me, they all say the same thing! Where is one to turn, for connection, for true memory?

Note; the like conduct of twin powers, Church and state, in time of crisis. Forced loyalty, machismo, sputterings of manhood, tests, taunts, calls to endurance, new credos. Obsessiveness, and its companionable opposite number, distraction of mind. Military metaphors virulently alive, in variation. Fear; of free play, vanity, lovemaking, celebration rites.

Something has so impregnated man's history, his conduct, as to be mistaken for history itself. Violence. In comparison, the "moral equivalent," is still unborn in him, a shadowy burden struggling for air and light and voice. We will not, in all likelihood, live to see this birth, to see the face of the newborn, the new man. Meantime, live as best we may, in "unacceptable communities," risky, edgy, even hunted down, kicked out of America.

Dostoevsky said the voice of Christ was intolerable to the Church, not to be borne, to be banished and extinguished. He sensed how amnesia opens up a division between word and act. One speaks and acts. But his act is not in accord with the word; it is in accord with his fear, his dread, hatred, the drag of his culture. The word is stifled in the hands of those who thought to protect it. So man is unable to purify, contradict, put to rights, rise from the dead.

The word is spoken finally, not as healing, but as a further alienating factor. Man is invited to forget—even as his salvation, as the way.

In such cases, the sense of mystery is progressively lost. Magical religion. Mystery as a vitalizing and radical act of remembrance is lost; the energy of a saving event is not released; man, taking the sacrament, does not submit to rebirth. He lies low, concealed under his idol-puppets, their maker and manipulator. The gods do his will and he names it worship. They offer only better and more seductive reasons to continue his rake's progress.

Remember your past! a counsel of elders to the young.

Often suspect; adults holding up for an ideal, the most absurd and destructive simulacrum of the past. The past recorded by victors, colonizers, slaveholders, the astute and sinister winners. A "worry stone" with the carven head of a pioneer or revolutionary; they efface the image in the worried task of keeping the peace, keeping the game legitimate.

The response of touch; turn away, wordless rejection, all the brimming disdain of affronted innocence, rage.

Re-member us. Put us together again, like broken dolls sprawling in the airless attic, the super ego, the locked and glutted storehouse of the rich. Connect thighbone to hipbone; make connections, re-member.

"*Membra disjecta*"; the slaughterhouse, the heroic battlefield. Hero, commoner, king, tossed in the common ditch, the glutted ossary of the powerful. Dismembered, un-remembered. String us together, tendon and marrow; another way.

A plenary consciousness, to remember one's brothers, a present concern, a presence. I am dismembered, disjointed, as long as hatred draws a line in the dust; thus far and no farther. Task: to widen the breadth of available communion. Danger: consciousness mobilized, brainwashed, "held in line," baited into battle. Then, the remembrance as we speak of becomes indictable activity. One is forbidden by law to remember his brother.

147

In bad times, religious symbols are often renewed by criminals. Cf. Paul, Villon, Quakers in Charles's England (hardly since), Hussites, Shakers, Anabaptists.

Luther, who almost remembered. Almost. Loyola, who remembered, whose disciples—forgot.

Culture as "amnesiac," a sleeping pill. It invariably lays a spell on the believer who swallows it.

The God of Israel "remembers not" the transgressions of men. Before Him, sins are as though they were not. In His compassion is man's healing. God and man by opposite activity (man remembers his sin, repents) are reconciled.

Remembering the future; an exercise in creation. A future comes to pass because here and now, one lives as though a future were possible.

Not any future at all. Not the brute unconscious extension of the present, a wheel that turns and turns, man bound to its fiery round. A breakthrough; myth of the chariot that took wing.

The nation required only some two hundred years to forget its revolution. Which is to say, to dismember its own body. Vietnam, Panthers, two aspects of autodismembering, a surgery of suicide.

Question: What Then Is It to Remember?
Answer: Forget It.

One thing you must grant our guru
    he is full of surprises as a Chinese new year
      or the brain of a guerrilla
firecrackers! disappearing acts! rambunction!
                             trompe l'oeil
      Just suppose . . . he continually says;
                         suppose . . .
     playing this way and that   the mind's
                        tight gear
erasing that ho-hum so stale as to leave a bad taste
      as of rank good wet parrot's feathers an
                    ogre aunt's dentures
      No. Just suppose . . .
"Enter into this renunciation, empty yourself
                  of forms
Be naked and void in oblivion and suspension."

Now such advice implies it   seems   to me a
                        substantial difficulty.
In the first place, the mystic too is a man   He
                        glories in it
    weighted down with pig iron   sand bags
                guyed by ropes and pulleys
arching over   firmly anchored   to terra firma
    A kind of circus tent   up there   down
        here   billowing   tugging
a stretched tegument   under which ALL KINDS
                                        OF
    OUTRAGEOUS CELEBRATION   exotic
                animals and men   take shelter
        do their breathtaking acts   grimace   mime
    break into snatches of immortal nonsense
    air their pied spirit
                O GRINS LIKE SILKEN PATCHES
        gleaming high on the royal American arses
        of chimps and men
    Our guru a   tent   I say
containing   like   a memory bank
    like fireflies in a park
        their stopped hearts   their held breaths
    the OHS and AHS   the indrawn HISS
        the sibilant   or round lipped   start of
                                        recognition
WE TOO ARE FLOWERS   BEASTS   CLOWNS
                                        CREATION
    creation!   its ineluctable concentrate   its drama
            in this airy breathing hive
    of gorgeous drones   sweating   brown jackets
while   under the sky   the invisible mystic queen
                coaxes   along   mothers   her dream
    brooding over   the egg and pith   cellular
        mystery & meaning of things
ARE WE THEN to empty the tent   to pull it

down   issuing against it
an ill tempered bailiff's warrant
forbidding on human precincts   necessary joys
brief accessible ecstasies?
REMEMBERING TOO (ironic use of a faculty
in very discussion of its useful blackout)
MEMORY is also the accumulated score of old ills
kept with a clerk's
scrupulous hand
from foul murders to farthings snatched from
blind beggars
and everything in between—
the score kept by god almighty man   I say
totting accounts   cramped in chains   writing in
dungeons
his code   indecipherable as a spider's brain
accounts "religiously" kept
the thick ledger   close mouthed as a shark
a doomsday book   one day to be opened!
Now are such memories to be abandoned
scattered
a cache of weapons laboriously assembled
blades   spikes
belaying   pins
bullets
against the day of retribution?
Memory   it must be confessed   is a very arsenal of
revolution
To void the menory   is   to betray our cache   to the
enemy of man
Granted
but it must also be pointed out
(In such dangerous matters   it is of utmost import
that no responsible voice be ignored)
Those who arm themselves from the arsenal of
memory

for whom crime must be repaid with crime
                    eye for eye   life for life
   in a most serious sense
                    risk capitulation
   to the malignant spirit
                    that from seats of power interminably
legitimates crime   as kings of old   legitimated their
                                             bastards
      Base born violence pollutes the bloodline of man
                                        interminably
      We shall never have done with it   until
                    we have done with it
      "Father forgive them   they know not what they
                                             do"
      A Fiction?   they knew quite well what they
                                             did
         they always know quite thoroughly
                         what they do
            which is to say
      FORGIVENESS
lies   in the greathearted choice of a man
            not neglectful of justice   no   not in his
                                      own case
         his skin being at least as dear to him
            as any other biped's
         No he is careful in his estimate of guilt (Not
                                      difficult;
it is incised in his own   he assembles the evidence
flesh, laid like blood   he adds it up
money on a butcher's   every jot and tittle
bench)   It is (he knows well)
                         as relevant to a just outcome
                         as a signed & sealed
                         confession
         NEVERTHELESS
         he puts   flame to the infamous paper

he scatters the traitorous money to the floor
declares; it is irrelevant to my cause
        (*my* cause underscored; the disposition of
                                    my life
            my chosen form of death
            the fate of my brothers)
    because he possesses his life he can give his life
He is not a gull he is no one's patsy
        He has not forgotton not for a moment
            the false friend who delivered him up
            the hand that grasped the lash
            the loutish arm that delivered the blows
            the hanging judge—
no it is all accounted for reckoned to a nicety

        reckoned and forgiven!
    This I judge is the act of forgetting
            of which the guru speaks
            the heart and nub of his argument:
        a radical transcending leap
            the transfiguring of wrongs their
                                    absorption
                in consciousness
    In somewhat this fashion a healthy man
            walks the plague ridden city His decision
                                    to live
        his being alive in a stew of death
                    is the vital consequence
        of his brothers' illness their despairing need
        of his skills hands heart his day to day
                                    level-eyed
            realism weighing his risk
        in the scales of their agony
                his own life
            at   dead center (live
center) that axis where existence both issues and
                                    returns

153

A question remains
Is such forgiveness historically useful
will it flush the foul stable
   of the accumulated crime
       of 9 buried cities?
Does forgiveness make the innocent
          less liable to assault battery murder
      I say it does when men are careful
                        to be neither
fools nor bloodletters
The decision to forgive crime in every instance to be
                             accompanied
          by the forced ousting of
      thugs time servers charlatans brutes
           from offices of power
Let the full account be drawn up of crimes against
                          the people
      knowing that the revolution is of human import
      in proportion as it issues from the just
                        estimate
          of violated justice

            But this is preliminary
   a clearing of decks for the auspicious voyage
Of course let the Eichmanns be confronted with
                        their crimes
      justice demands it the blood of the victims
                    cries out for it
          but not no by no act of vengeance

      the revolution is of human import
   in proportion as it creates
      new ways of dealing with Eichmanns
rather than the old condign exactions
      they (and we) are so lethally skilled in

A *Penny Primer in the Art of Forgetfulness*

What is the price of attaining the future?
Forgetting the future

What is the price of revolution?
Forgetting the revolution

What things are to be forgotten?
The good things

Only?
Also the evil things

All things?
All things

What good things for instance?
Father mother family friends

also books   tastes   a settled abode
the view at the window
ecstasy   flowers
the turn and tide of season

What bad things?
Offenses   hurts   foolishness   also
instinctive lunges   settled enmities
termites   rank offenses   shark mouths
the stuttering etc of nightmare

What is the value of this?
Connection

Where will it lead?
Forget where it will lead

You ask me to become a boor
an aardvark   an amputee?
No.   A man

How a man?
A man is one enabled
to forget
both method and way
He is consumed
in the act & grace of manhood
the entire gift

What gift act grace?
We must borrow
one outlawed debased word
love

And then?
Then then then

Run off   empty your mind
like a dawn slops
or I shall I swear
by the Zen fathers
thwack your dense shoulders
with this bamboo

"Night Darkens the Soul of Man: but Only to Illuminate It" Words Once More Taken from the Notes of Our Guru

This night darkens the spirit but only to illuminate it
                                                        afterward
with respect to all things
this night humbles the spirit renders it without joy
but only to raise it up and exalt it
it impoverishes the spirit deprives it
but only to enable it to arise
in unfettered freedom of spirit to perfect fruition
of all things in heaven and on earth
Then in a new purity the spirit tastes the sweetness
                                                of all things
in a pre-eminent and sublime manner

The light imparted to the man   who undergoes this night
transcends every light of nature
and cannot be grasped by the understanding

If then the mind of man is to be united with this light
and to become divine
it must first be purged and annihilated
with respect to its natural light
and led into darkness
When this has been done
the divine light and illumination   will take the place
of the natural mode and manner of understanding
Moreover
in order to attain to the union
to which this dark night is leading a man
he must be filled with a certain glorious splendor
The prophet says it;
No eye has seen   no ear has heard
nor has it entered into the heart of man to conceive
what God has prepared for those who love him.
This is why a man must first become empty and poor
and purged from all natural support
so that   in total poverty of spirit
he may live that new and blessed life

At times
everything appears so strange and unaccustomed to such a
                                                    man
that he feels enchanted   or in a trance
He goes about marveling at the things he hears and sees
even though nothing is different
from what he saw or heard before
Such a man is becoming estranged
from ordinary ways of thinking and knowing
so that   in dying to these
he may be filled with new knowledge and love

Furthermore
in this night of contemplation
he is being prepared
for inner tranquillity and peace
so profound and blissful
as to surpass all understanding

For this reason man must abandon all former peace
which full of imperfection as it was
could not be named peace at all
He must be purged of that "peace"
He must be stirred up and relinquish his false peace
This experience causes such deep pain a man
sometimes cries aloud in spiritual agony

This strife is fought out
in the deepest parts of the soul
because the peace for which such a man strives
is most deep and interior
The pain of such a man is inward and all pervasive
because the love for which he strives
will be equally intimate and pure

Some Definitions of Favorite Recurring Words of Our Guru Are Now in Order

BEGINNER (op., expert) Just about any mortal, awakening to any morning in the world's history. Including the morning after death. First thought: where the hell am I? Second thought: why?

INWARDNESS Quality of wells, cisterns, ears, tombs, bellies. Used sometimes as synonyms for hunger, stillness, waiting; as of eyes before dawn, brides before lovers. Cf. the Buddhist "tao." A complete, nearly universal sense, variously named "religious," "mystical," "human," is attested to by numerous saints, savants, poets and (in the West) newly qualified "bums." VIRTUE. There is no extant mythology attesting to the frugality or industry of

Buddha. Jesus (cf. Gospels *passim*) was a notorious free-loader. The Upanishads are interestingly empty of such sayings as relate to "laying aside goods for a rainy day," "a stitch in time," "bread on the waters," etc., etc.; which sayings must rather be traced to the spinning and cunning of puritan drudges, of much later date and more questionable cultures. Likewise with private property. The gurus, presuming free legitimate access to earth, air, fire, water, variously occupied, drank, breathed, and retired to these, occasion offering. They dwelt in remote places, like sticks and stones and clouds, giving not a damn as to the indemnities, posts, fences, electric eyes, guards, fines or prisons attached throughout history to such trespassers, loiterers, saunterers, disturbers of purported peace. There, dwelling immobile, in caves or under the beat of the sun, they were gradually transformed (cf. above) into wells, cisterns, ears, tombs, bellies. And filled. Subsequent history might, from one point of view, be considered as a long procession of searching men, moving in this direction, to drink, to hear, to eat, to be reborn. There is, to the present day, no perceptible diminution of this phenomenon.

BLINDLY BELIEVE "Do not, anyone, anything" might be understood as the sigilla of modern man; a consequence of his having been "taken" too often, for everything he owns. The saying was coined, it has been surmised, in the depths of an ash can; where consigned by con men, social engineers, genetic accident or Providence, man awaits his apotheosis.

Another theory however strongly contradicts the foregoing; it traces the cultural origins of the oppression to the European thirties, when the upraised enticing arms, marmoreal jaw, enchanting mustache, infallible oracles of political strong men drew millions of restless spirits to urban squares and their chancery balconies, on which were re-enacted ancient cults first devised by imperial rulers B.C. In this theory, the massing of "blind believers," led with all speed to "creation-destruction" rituals that followed.

The expression, whatever its origin, is total and totalizing. A difficulty arises; the gods are both numerous and vociferous. The "true God," on whose existence a few misfits, poets, malcontents, cretins, resisters, indentured servants, condemned criminals, etc., etc., have persistently staked what they refer to as "everything," is, by hypothesis, One; and by preference, silent. Thus the evidence for his existence is embarrassingly meager. To "blindly believe" in this context, must be named an act of altogether unprecedented folly, hedged about with condign punishment. Still, some do. To this day. Driven and seized upon by what demons, blinded by what inner absurdity, modern psychology is still in process of unraveling.

There is a saying in this regard, which arose in the course of a late series of mass executions; "What a fool the god of the fools must be!" A highly placed official of the state, addressing the multitudes in the arena, spoke with acid scorn of "the Transcendent Fool," holding foolish court, decked out in cap and bells, attended by a hirsute, filthy, hunkering crowd of noisy agitators bent on the destruction of public order, flaunting the decency of good men, etc., etc. His words received unprecedented ovations.

The day following, in every temple of the nation, purificatory rites were held, including the symbolic burning with newly struck fire, of the baptismal records of any who had committed crimes against the state, whether by showing disrespect to national emblems, speaking with disparagement of public officials, or refusing to serve in the armed forces of the nation. The rite of purification was held outside the church walls to symbolize the excommunication of criminal elements.

There followed a lengthy procession of re-entrance. In the nation's capital, the rite was enacted with singular reverence and splendor. The chief priest presided, bearing the national flag through the square on a silken pillow. Accompanied by the President and attended by the Joint Chiefs of Staff, his eminence, Priest XXIX, passed into the great nave of the National Cathedral and advanced alone to the high altar, where he draped the outspread flag over the Exalted Cross. The ceremony closed with the chanting, by massed choir and congregation of the national anthem, "Blindly Believe."

DISCIPLE. A religionist (cf. above)
Conversely, a "loser" (cf. also above)

In either case, an evidence of the human disposition to seek out symbols, signs, wonders, portents, gurus (cf. also Browning; "a man's reach is longer than his arm; else what's a heaven for?")

Presupposes "giving one's self"; a formula which raises more questions, possibly, than it answers. Such as; to what, for what?

Related also; "discipline," q.v.

PARABLE. Long way home. The mind, traveling not as the crow flies, but in "descending gyres." Invariable method of Jesus, Isaiah, Thurber, La Fontaine, etc. Invariable formulas: "Once there was a . . ." "Once upon a time . . ." allow the mind breathing space, to take soundings, sniff about, get bearings.

All creation is grist for this mill. No main lines of development are susceptible to credible analysis. The outrageous, innovative character of this method is a clue to its subversive potential; as realized by nation states. Cf. one recent decree: "Subtle purveyors of disorder and discontent to be plucked from the nation's hearths." The life expectancy of such spinners of dreams is not great. The mysterious question of the survival of the species, among Basques, gypsies, Navahos, Taoists, etc., therefore also arises.

The absolute and universal vindication of ideological purity is not however seriously challenged by the existence of such types, since in almost every instance, those accused in the above matter have been adequately dealt with.

WISDOM The look in old eyes (young eyes) as of distant mountains when one stands upon flatlands; springs in a desert where no twig has bent. What makes the unbearable to be borne.

Sometimes present when presumed absent; as by hints, starts, somehows, nonethelesses, never-minds. Simultaneous with the dumb hope in the eyes of Mother Hubbard's dog, to whom the absence of bones in cupboards is by no means catastrophic, nor, upon proof of which dearth, all bets are off with the deceiving world. It being the magnanimous quality of such insight, curling up uncosseted to sleep, to reflect within its dog's brain; the Bone that was not, still walks.

CONFUSION In Greek myth, the rich original batter and mix of all differentiated creation. That out of which. Also, within which; sink, swim. Quality possibly the quality most abhorred, renounced, denounced, roundly assailed, by politicos on the make. Conversely; assiduously packaged, vended, consumed by the electorate. Cf. the skilled prestidigitation by the former, resulting in the admiring judgment by the latter: "Well, he has access to all the facts and I don't."

To be born of which is both honorable and inevitable, as, e.g., a noble French crêpe.

To remain in which is ruinous and indeed against the course of nature, as the self-willed, unborn, drown in their own juice and element.

PETITION The addressing of power by the powerless, operative within an old classic assumption; to wit, power is in principle benign; attention paid the powerless is the *raison d'être* of power in the first place.

When times were good, God was supposed to listen; the times in a sense, made it easy for him. When times were bad, men were not so sure. The faith of many fell away.

When times were good, however, one could not conclude automatically to an increase of faith. That would be too easy, as theologians pointed out. It remained true that people tended to tilt back their chairs and simply enjoy. In certain cultures at such times, bullfights became all the rage.

The bulls seldom won.

In bad times, on the other hand, there was notable increase in animal births. Bull calves tended to be more numerous than females. (A correlation is difficult to establish.) The bulls also won more often over the matadors, who seemed overanxious, and made false moves. If anyone prayed at such times (the prayer of petition, that is), it was the mothers of bullfighters.

On the political scene, good times were defined by the wars we won. But good times or bad, Americans were frequently reminded that Americans had never lost a war. Perhaps the only index to good times or bad, in this regard, was at some times leaders more frequently reminded the public of this fact. There was as well the question of the oath, taken with some heat, to the effect that the present incumbent was not going to be the first President to preside over such an event. He was, invariably, not. The wars went on. If we did not win, we certainly did not lose.

LAW That which violated brings down the present order. That which obeyed makes one the instrument of order maintained. That which, beyond scrutiny or critique, is a gift of the gods; indeed a guaranteed gilt-edged share in predestination. That which is self-evident, on the face of things. No matter what happens next door, no matter whose door is pounded down, no matter who dragged off. No matter what wars, no matter what methods. No matter. The matter is aired in public courts and vindicated in private prisons, where, most privately, recalcitrants are granted time and place for rehabilitation. Which when demonstrated beyond reasonable doubt to have occurred, the malfeasant is reunited with decent men. The matter was considered closed. The wars (presuming a war in question) go on.

DEVIL He whose entrance to the national gardens is (as of present writing) efficiently blocked by the Immigration Control Act of the late 40s.

BOETHIUS Ancient, savant, said, "If you wish to know truth with the lucidity of nature, cast out fear, hope, joy and sorrow." Since discredited.

SCRIPTURES The word of God in whatever language or tradition. Opened by dint of inspiration or chance, to any given page, they might advise one to start a war, to desist from war, to build a temple, to gut a temple, to die for others, to violate others, etc., etc. At best, a luminous minoritarian summation of the wall of God for the heroic few. At worst, no worse than the unexpressed longings of the majority of men, who frequently consult such oracles, expecting a blessing on the conduct and expectancies of the imperial method. And invariably get it, necessity in this case being the sedulous mother of invention.

The chosen people turn to this source to be assured of who they are, the rejects are told to buck up; advice which they badly need and render due thanks for, returning on Monday to labor in house or field, or wherever assigned.

Now and again, losers have claimed to find in the scrolls a hint or promise of revolution, as though God too were fed up with the stench of things. Such men are dealt with as their crime deserves, usually with the blessing of the Keepers of the Scrolls, whom even scandal-mongers hardly ever accuse of special pleading.

VISION That without which (*vide* above) the people die. (Competent scholarship has judged the text probably corrupt.)

JOY A natural spontaneous overflow; *élan vitale* amok. Associated with the right time, place and event; as children at kiteflying, roses responding to benign weather, men and women to roses. The slight upturn of the mouth observed in humans, usually bent upon mischief against public order; thereafter carved in pumpkins, by whose instruction or what convention no one has discovered: So that, candles being lighted and placed within, the natural universe may radiate, from its molten center, some rare spontaneous epiphany of man. By grant or by design, no man may easily say. Scarcely a man is found who cares to say.

IMAGINATION Highly touted faculty; classic literature both praises its splendor and puts it on display, like a loquacious peacock in a nuptial dance. Today all but extinct; residual traces in remote peoples are the object of anthropological expeditions and taping sessions with natives.

Functioned, as far as can be reconstructed, with what were named "alternatives." These appeared in painted images, verses, dance, religious rites, all bodying forth the inner rhythms by which men, in spite of the brute world and their own evil, hoped on.

The above reflections are of course conjectural. A cave painting found on the long island situated outside the ruins of Noue Yurk, is probably the most striking evidence of the last phase of this art. Men there "imagined," with

169

a kind of sublime crudity, a utopian city free of smog, filth and crowding; a transcendent figure breathes his blessing on the people from above. The cave, thought to be an ancient transport station, is open to visitors.

One can only note the inevitable "extinction by decree" of this faculty, rendered obsolete by necessities of public order and polity. There followed shortly the psychological transmutation known as the "great sleep"; the law thereafter evolved by the Schaldt school, has had incalculable import for education, law, medicine and treatment of deviants; "If man has no need of ——, it no longer exists."

GRACE (Gr., xaris—gift, favor) Neoclassicists were fond of picturing the ineffable visitants in human form; usually as females diaphanously clad, performing a spring dance.

Under the hypothesis that gods existed, such images cannot be automatically judged decadent.

Later value-free cultures could not easily tolerate their continuance, as images corresponding to reality.

The "Humanization of Domestic Man" campaign, following on the "pacification of Foreign Tribes" campaign, rendered such concepts obsolete. Certain images of earlier periods are on permanent exhibit at the National Museum Against Religion, Folklore and Hypocrisy.

Two Texts Are Commended by Our Guru as Commending a Reasonable Freedom from the Goods and Services of This World

One is not thereby left hanging in the void; he is rather inundated with other goods, other services. Still of this world, but yet of another. But let us look at the texts. The first is taken from an old letter, written by another guru to his people.
As servants of God we commend ourselves in every way through great endurance
in affliction   hardships   calamities
beatings   imprisonments   tumults
labors   watchings   hunger
by purity   knowledge   forbearance   kindness

the Holy Spirit   genuine love
truthful speech   and the power of God
with the weapon of justice on the right hand and the left
in honor and dishonor
in ill repute and good repute
We are treated as impostors   and yet speak the truth
as despised and yet honored
as dying   and behold we live
as punished   and yet not perishing
as sorrowful   and yet rejoicing
as poor   yet enriching many
as having nothing   yet possessing all things
Our mouth is open to you brothers   our heart is wide
In return   widen your hearts also

Whenever I have the courage to return it, I find the
text a literal source of energy. Why, I cannot be sure. But
it has something to do, I suspect, with the insight that
John of the Cross enlarges on; to cut free from the things
men ordinarily give their hearts to, is not to lose the world,
or the hearts of others, or the moral complicity with the
fate of others which is all our longing and very nearly all
our fate. No, it is to regain these things in a new way.

It is to enter more dramatically and fully into the truth
of things, which always appears to men under one or another guise. On the one hand, as a sinister and brutal
struggle, a tangle in which one, willy-nilly is caught; from
which there is no true relief except death itself. And on
the other, as a struggle also, of the most frightful nature
and scope; but one in which the outcome, despite all ap-
pearances, threats, powers and dominions, wounds and set-

backs, is clearly on the side of the good; on the side of good men. Faith in God, that is to say, does nothing to blunt or stifle one's sense of evil in the world. Quite to the contrary; it sharpens that sense, almost beyond endurance. But it confers, at the same time, what I can only call a sense beyond that sense of things. What one can only call, a "mediate" sense of evil, of its penultimate character. Evil reigns for a while, it cannot have the last word—either in regard to the direction of the universe, or the fate of man.

I am not sure how well believers have dealt with a vision which was always at their disposal. Or rather, perhaps I know too well; they have been cowards and killers, they have been overwhelmed by evil, they have run from it, made pacts with it, welcomed it into their dwellings. Which is to say, on the *tabula rasa* of history they have not notably impressed the mark of unique vision, of special or heroic virtue. Still, a few of them have; and one of these was the writer of the above-quoted letter.

And he spells out the consequences: eminently concrete, immediate, attractive even, in their wide range of exposure to weathers, to fortune, to conflict, to the eye of event. I like that. I like the tightrope which he thereupon walked. The figure is limited of course by the constant tactile sense he conveys, not of being far above the scene, daring space and gravity; but grounded, so to speak, so that his high-wire act becomes a matter of the most daring, unexpected, and skillful moral choices.

He gained a greater measure of life, by freeing his life for action. He set up the possibility for a heightening of drama; he teased and tested himself and others; almost as

173

though the life of his soul was to be discovered to himself, only if he consistently set himself the most unlikely, dreaded or despised task, encounters, projects; entered upon them, saw their whole course through, and afterward reflected (ruefully, joyfully) on the next step. Something has been gained, something lost, but in any case, something learned. He could go from there, with the growth of soul, insight, purpose, courage which his spirit had accreted to itself.

I do not know a more admirable way in which to grow in freedom. Nor do I know any account which stands as a stronger reproof to the corrupt claim known today in academic circles and elsewhere, as "value-free" intelligence. For Paul (as for John, I would think) the concept is not only despicable, dragged in as it so often is to mask one's real intent, one's actual method. At depth, it violates the law by which man's spirit functions; in virtue of a tradition, that is, in the wrestling and conflict of one's values with actual life.

I have heard the universities declare themselves in principle, as value free; usually in opposition to those who insist that political or moral views be debated, aired, arrived at, on campuses. Hands are raised in horror against the suggestion. The university, in embracing this or that political choice, would only become a bloody field of conflict, renege on its intellectual vocation, be trodden down by the same forces that make shambles of quiet streets, or peaceable homes, of the churches. . . .

One does not mean to deny the complexity of a given question, when he points out that complexity is also a form of special pleading much beloved by those to whose interest it is, that no solutions be arrived at.

"Value free"; a mirage is always conjured up by the phrase; the sweeping lawns of rustic academe, earnest scholars in well-appointed secular-monastic dwellings, pondering the images, types, metaphors of the universe; their mind's juices, fermenting in vats of the spirit, seeping into the world through a hundred conduits of art, science, numbers, rhythms, voices . . . Freed from the encumbrances and toils of commoners, set aside for special rigors, a vowed chastity of purpose and mind; men to whose ears the tumult of empire, of ambition, of hatreds and violence, are in their sum, less than the beat of a distant sea. . . .

Hogwash. Everything else aside, the university as a corporate body is about as value free as say, the Pentagon. Its monies come to it, not from value-free financiers, but from their world or domestic predators, the robber barons of the twentieth century, who also according to most university charters, control university decisions. To put it crudely, they buy a slice of the action, large or small, according to appetite and the going market. They in turn, in concert with department heads, research heads, specialists of every ilk, investment experts, etc., play both sides of certain Washington avenues, where national interest is sold to bidders, who contract in various ways, for the furtherance, widening, and extension of same. Voilà!

Now we are free if we will, to yield for a moment to the vision of a filmy-eyed dreamer, visionary, his tweeds and pipe, his ivory tower, his archeology, his Rosetta stones, his Babylonian lore . . . What would all this fury, this game, this low politicking, mean to him?

Even granting his existence, his innocence, his irrelevance, we may still be forgiven for pointing out that the value-free life and research of such a spirit are joined (university rhetoric has always joined him) to a larger community, which in turn, is linked to the above pursuits, bargains—values, in sum.

The case rests; enough said. Let us remark only the remarkably sane and constant unity of spirit, which joins Paul to John, and both perhaps to our own sense of things. It is a great and good thing, *dignum et justum*, when one's life is so impregnated with the values of a tradition, his life so colored, so impelled, so led as to be able to wrestle with the demons of his own (and others') lifetime. We shall see who emerges from the labyrinth; the minotaur or the man.

Let a Man Ground His Joy and Love in That Which He Neither Sees Nor Feels Nor Can Feel or See in This Life: Namely in God.

Now the above, I thought, had the virtue of putting the matter baldly. The virtue of a plain-speaking, courageous surgeon of the soul! Whose only fear, if he had to admit to one, would be that of deceiving another.

I remember the astonishment of a good friend, when I answered, to the question of what this underground existence (then some three months along in parturition) meant or might mean. I answered: it means I am learning to pray. Which is cutting the matter, cleanly, and to the bone. There is a dynamic of the spirit, which I want to set in motion, in a desiccated and desperate time, when the

177

measure of man is commonly taken according to the most stereotyped and sinister images; the well- or mal-functioning robot, the obedient cretin, the lobotomized victim.

I wanted something else to pay the high price of being conscious. Freud, young Luther, Gandhi, Jesus, Socrates; we have set our sights too low and too near to include these burning lights, who wandered the city of the dead, and called men into being once more.

My brother, Philip, meditating in prison; myself, meditating in someone's attic room; we have done something more downright than turn our backs on bad politics or the evil of men. We are trying to get reborn. Or to put the matter more exactly, to allow the conditions of rebirth free play. To stand apart from the crushing weight of distraction, affluence and corrupt reward which is the reward and revenge of the world on those who fight the world with its own weapons or scramble up its pointless ladders.

Bear with me, if I seem too harsh for comfort. I am first of all too harsh for my own comfort; some consolation for those who read this, and conclude that middle-aged acedia is the juice I swim in.

No, it has been a question induced by the very push of circumstance, of the search for a space to be man in, how deep one must cast the roots of life, before there can be reasonable guarantee that his harvest will not be another lethal seductive fruit in the spoiled garden.

I took the present task to be one of contemplation. I was not in flight from the society, but in pursuit of its lost and neglected truth. Where this would lead, how far, in what direction, with what outcome, or what public "usefulness" I could not know; in the nature of things. Any more than any condemned outcast, bent upon turning a wrong definition of his life into a right one, and so recovering his soul.

Such a definition, could not be applied externally, like a coat of paint on a ruined surface. No, it was a question of verifying one's existence, of renewing the springs and roots of life. Otherwise, under the new "name" the old surface would continue to rot and fall away. One does not argue himself, by whatever hidden persuasion, into rebirth.

To achieve this, time would be of the essence. My friends largely missed this point. The supposition seemed to be that one had to have his days filled with something known as "meaningful activity"—meetings, secret trips to other towns, a barrage of "exposure" (the sexual implication here is a delight) to the media. One is evidently terrified of the vacuum, the yawn of time, the burdensome memories of old friends, connections, works and pomps, the "dolce vita," long gone but not forgotten. The clean break was not to be my skill; misfortune in men's eyes had to be relieved by all the sops and visual and auditory aids at our common disposal. Let the bad news be kept at all cost from the patient.

Whereas, I was refusing the analogy, as applying in my case. Illness, wounds, loneliness, alienation were not the point—which was, to any right sense of things, brutal and even final. Something more like: have mercy on your friend; respect his wish, and let him die.

Theatrical? I hope not. I wanted, like Vergil or Ivan Illyich or Socrates, a space, a measure of time in which to

179

prepare for death; for that integration of my soul which might approach death as a living man rather than a walking zombie; and for what that hour might include.

To "include"; not to go into that hour in a suicidal way, however nobly intended, but as a man alive to the unknown, the release, the newness that might possibly accompany all that blood and dolor. Perhaps, a newborn cry.

I remember Thomas Merton writing me about a year before his death, somewhat in this vein, with his own mix of the playful and grotesquerie. I am already dead, dead, he declared. I am already dead, only they haven't discovered it yet. When they do, they will undoubtedly bury me with honors; for the present, I go around with all the business of living, playing a part. But everything is gone.

I think I know what he was driving at. With regard to most of our fellows in Church and state, both my brother and I are really dead men. It makes no sense not to start with that fact. We have no stake in Church or state, as currently in evidence; their aims, their values, their mutual transfusions of comfort. We have said no to it all. And more than this: for our "no" has been taken at its word. What else can I conclude, when he sweats out a felon's day in high-security prison, when the sedulous hounds are hot on my trail? No, we can never complain that we have not been taken seriously . . .

And what of the Church? There, we are taken seriously too. *Aus mit.* Even if we are tolerated, the tolerance has little of virtue about it; in a time of public irrational upheaval, we are simply another instance of those who fly the coop, kick over traces, or anticwise, hang around to make trouble. In any case, we are never to be taken seriously; never to become the occasion of rebirth, renunciation of wealth, conversion of heart. We are never invited to be heard from; we never count for much. This is the sentence, passed *in absentia*. It is the reduction of the living to the remote acre of the dead.

Did we once think we would count for something; or that suffering repression, the threat or actuality of personal harm, we would win the attention of our fellow Christians, of our fellow priests? alas and alas. When Philip was cast into solitary confinement and began his fast, we could not think (as one would instinctively think), now they will listen, now they will protest, now they will speak up for him! No such thing; our hope was extinguished. We must appeal, across all lines, to the good sense and compassion of all our friends, including of course, a few fellow Catholics, a few priests. But the attention of the Great Church was as usual, fixated on the Great Society.

We are dead to all that.

Someday, wrote Merton, they will discover that I am already dead.

When one comes to this truth, as to a still center of existence, he quite possibly has become a man of prayer. What is certain, is that such a realization gives me an inkling, however fleeting and mazed, of the fate of human goodness in a bad time.

Men normally win the kind of eternity for which their lives prepare them, Socrates said to his friends. Indeed.